Your Food Is Fooling You

How Your Brain Is Hijacked by Sugar, Fat, and Salt

Your Food Is Fooling You

How Your Brain Is Hijacked by Sugar, Fat, and Salt

David A. Kessler, MD

Adapted by Richie Chevat *from* The End of Overeating

Roaring Brook Press / New York

Copyright © 2013 by David A. Kessler

Published by Roaring Brook Press

Roaring Brook Press is a division of Holtzbrinck Publishing Holdings Limited Partnership

175 Fifth Avenue, New York, New York 10010

Published by arrangement with Rodale Inc. Adapted from *The End of Overeating: Taking Control of the Insatiable American Appetite* by David Kessler, MD.

macteenbooks.com

Library of Congress Cataloging-in-Publication Data

Kessler, David A., 1951–
    Your food is fooling you : how your brain is hijacked by sugar, fat,
and salt / David A. Kessler : adapted by Richie Chevat. — 1st ed.
        p. cm.
    Includes index.
    ISBN 978-1-59643-831-6
    1. Nutrition—Psychological aspects.   2. Obesity—Prevention—United
States.   3. Health behavior—United States.   I. Chevat, Richie.   II. Title.
    QP151.K47 2013
    613.2—dc23

                                                            2012032020

Roaring Brook Press books are available for special promotions and premiums.
For details contact: Director of Special Markets, Holtzbrinck Publishers.

First Edition 2012
Printed in the United States of America
10 9 8 7 6 5 4 3 2 1

CONTENTS

PART THREE
UNDERSTANDING OVEREATING

PART FOUR
FOOD REHAB

PART ONE

SUGAR, FAT, SALT

CHAPTER 1

What Is *Overeating*?

I got the idea to write this book while watching a daytime talk show. On the show a psychologist was talking about why so many Americans are overweight. He asked for a volunteer from the audience. A large, well-dressed woman named Sarah stood up. The psychologist asked Sarah to talk about her problems with weight.

At first Sarah was all smiles. "I eat all the time," she said with a nervous giggle. "I eat when I'm hungry; I eat when I'm not hungry. I eat when I'm happy; I eat when I'm sad."

Then the psychologist asked Sarah to describe how she felt about herself.

The sunny smile on her face faded. Sarah said she felt like a failure. She called herself "fat" and "ugly." She said that she ate too much even though she knew it wasn't good for her. Afterward, she often felt angry with herself for not being able to stop.

"I feel that I can't do it," she said, choking back tears. "That I don't have the willpower. My whole thought is about why I eat, what I eat, when I eat, with whom I eat," she said. "I don't like myself."

The psychologist asked how many in the audience had ever felt like that. About two-thirds of them raised their hands. They all had a problem with *overeating*.

Eating Is Making Us Sick

I use the term *overeating* a lot in this book. You've probably never heard of overeating before, but I bet you know what I mean. Too many Americans are just eating way too much. We're eating more than our bodies need. All that extra food gets turned into fat.

And it is making us sick.

About one-third of all adults in the United States are overweight. Another third are *obese*. That means they are not just overweight, but extremely overweight. Being obese leads to many health problems, including diabetes, heart disease, and some kinds of cancers. Taken together, that means that two-thirds of Americans weigh more than they should to be healthy.

This is very personal for me because I am one of those Americans who has struggled with weight and overeating. I have lost weight, gained it back, and lost it again—over and over and over. I have owned suits in every size. When I heard Sarah on that TV show, I knew exactly what she was talking about.

I'm a doctor and I have often wondered why so many people, including myself, have so much trouble with eating. It's natural to eat when you're hungry. It's also natural to *stop* eating when you're full. Yet something is turning off the natural switch in our brains that tells us to stop eating.

That's what I call *overeating*. It's when people eat all the time, whether or not they're hungry. It's when people feel they have lost control and have to eat no matter how bad it is for them.

A Problem for Kids, Too

Overeating is a big problem for kids, too. Like grownups, more and more kids just never stop eating. That means that more and more kids are gaining dangerous amounts of weight.

About 17 percent or more than 12 million kids aged two to nineteen are obese. Another 12 million are overweight. That means that 34 percent, or more than one-third of all young Americans, weigh too much.

A strange part of the overeating problem is that many thin people struggle with it, too. These people may not be obese, but they spend all day thinking about food, tempted to eat. Eating or not eating becomes a constant battle for them. Instead of something to enjoy, food becomes their enemy, something they have to fight against. At the other end of the spectrum are eating disorders where people become fearful of food or try too hard to control what they eat. That's not good, either.

If you're young and you're not overweight, you may not even think about this. You may be consuming snacks like candy or high sugar "energy" drinks all day long without even realizing it. You may be eating super-size portions that you don't need. In other words, you may already be *overeating* without knowing it. You may not be overweight now, but if you develop the habit of overeating when you are young, you are going to have problems with eating later in life.

Being aware of the dangers of overeating is the best way to make sure you don't have to struggle with food for the rest of your life.

Overeating Everywhere

Once I started looking around, I saw people overeating everywhere. It wasn't hard to spot. I'd see people in restaurants, lifting food to their mouths, even though they hadn't finished chewing the last bite. When their plates were empty, they'd reach across the table to spear a french fry or bite of dessert from someone else's plate.

I realized that everywhere I looked, people were *always eating*. People ate while walking down the street. They ate while sitting in their cars. They ate all day long, during meals, between meals, whenever they could.

But why? And why couldn't they stop? The answer to that question is what this book is about.

You Are the Target

What I discovered is that overeating is not happening by accident. Americans did not all decide to just start eating nonstop. We did not suddenly lose our "willpower" or become weak. We overeat largely because of the way food is now manufactured and marketed. Foods are designed and sold to us in ways that *make us want to eat more*.

What foods are these? You probably know the answer. Some are foods like sweetened drinks, chips and cookies, candy, and other snack foods. Then, of course, there are fast food meals—fried chicken, pizza, burgers, and fries. And there are thousands of other processed foods like frozen dinners and breakfast cereals and "energy drinks" and more.

A lot of this processed food is marketed to young people. Fast food restaurants, high-energy drinks, candy bars, and other snacks are all heavily advertised to teens. You may even have candy and soda vending machines in your school. Your school cafeteria may be serving this highly processed food.

Food companies make these foods with very large amounts of three ingredients—sugar, fat, and salt. Let me repeat that because it's important:

☞ Sugar, Fat, and Salt

These three ingredients, when put together in the right amounts, *make us eat more*. Think about that. Instead of satisfying our hunger, these foods train our bodies and our brains to want more. And food companies, including fast food chains, understand this very well. They are hard at work to make new foods that will get us to keep eating.

The End of Overeating

One of the most important things I've learned is that we don't have to be afraid of food. Foods that come to us without added sugar, salt, and fat are healthy and delicious—and they do not make us overeat. We can enjoy eating foods like fruits, vegetables, whole grains, fish, and meat as long as they don't have added sugar, fat, and salt.

For some people, overeating may not be a problem. But if you're already eating snacks throughout the day, plus eating super-sized portions at every meal, then you are going to have to learn a new way of eating. It takes some time and practice to retrain your brain. But the good news is that it can be done. The first step is to understand why some foods make us crave more food. Then you can learn how to stop the cravings.

Once you've done that, you can stop worrying about food. You'll eat when you're hungry and enjoy your meals without feeling bad.

I hope reading this book helps you as much as writing it helped me.

CHAPTER 2

America Gained Weight

Americans are overweight. I'd be surprised if you haven't heard that dozens of times. Maybe you learned it in school or saw a report on the news, or maybe you've seen shows like *The Biggest Loser* on TV.

☞ **More than two-thirds of all adult Americans are either overweight or obese.**

Sometimes, when we hear the same thing over and over, we start to tune out. But the news about Americans and weight is something we can't afford to ignore. Here's how serious it is: As of 2008, 68 percent of adult Americans were either overweight or obese. As I pointed out in the previous chapter, that's more than two-thirds of the country!

Why is this so serious? Because being overweight or obese leads to serious health problems. Here are some of the diseases caused by being overweight:

- Heart disease
- Type 2 diabetes
- Some types of cancers
- High blood pressure
- High cholesterol
- Stroke
- Liver and gallbladder disease
- Breathing problems
- Arthritis
- Infertility

It's not just adults. As I mentioned earlier, one-third of all American kids are either overweight or obese. That includes babies and toddlers under the age of five. Kids who are obese are more likely to grow up to be obese adults. They are on track to have one or more of the diseases just listed. For example, type 2 diabetes used to unheard of among children. Today, more and more kids are getting this disease.

• • • • • • • • • • • • • • • •

▶ OVERWEIGHT VS. OBESE ◀

What's the difference between *overweight* and *obese*? Overweight means you weigh more than is healthy for you. Obese means you are very overweight. Obese people are much more likely to have serious health problems like diabetes, heart disease, high blood pressure, and some kinds of cancer.

It is healthy to have some fat in your body. You just don't want to have too much. What is a healthy weight? There's no single number that fits everyone. Your healthy weight will depend on your height, your age, and whether you are a boy or a girl.

• • • • • • • • • • • • • • • • •

▶ WHAT IS DIABETES? ◀

Your body produces a hormone called insulin. Insulin controls the level of glucose (sugar, carbohydrates) in the blood. A lack of insulin is called type 1 diabetes. A block in insulin action is called type 2 diabetes. Obesity interferes with insulin action and can lead to type 2 diabetes.

Both type 1 and type 2 diabetes, if not treated, result in high levels of blood sugar and cholesterol. Over time, deposits of glucose and cholesterol accumulate in blood vessels and nerves and lead to heart disease, stroke, blindness, kidney failure, and gangrene. Eighty percent of heart attacks are due to diabetes. Most amputations of feet and legs are the result of diabetes, and diabetes is the seventh leading cause of death in the United States.

• • • • • • • • • • • • • • • • •

It Wasn't Always Like This

You've grown up in a world where many people are overweight. You might think this is just a fact of life. Many adults also believe this. They think it's just natural that many people are overweight and obese. They believe it's just natural to gain a lot of weight as we get older.

But this is not true. We know it's not true because until about 30 years ago, there were *very few* obese Americans.

That's right. Until just a short time ago, we did not have a weight problem in America. In fact, throughout history, for thousands of years, human body weight stayed pretty much the same. Yes, there were some people who were obese or overweight, but most people had no trouble with their weight. They ate the amount of food they needed and no more.

Then, in the 1980s, something changed. Americans started gaining weight—a lot of it.

Katherine Flegal was one of the first scientists to see what was happening. She worked for the U.S. government. Around 1991, she was studying the results of a government survey of Americans. What she saw was so surprising she didn't believe it at first. The numbers showed that one-third of all adult Americans were overweight.

This was a very big change, and it had happened very quickly. In fewer than 12 years, about 20 million people had become overweight. The change was so big and so fast that

Flegal thought she must have made a mistake. She and her team went back and checked and double-checked. But the results were the same. A huge number of Americans had become overweight in a short time.

Flegal's team published its report. Then other researchers came up with the same results. In every group they studied, men and women, young and old, black and white, they found the same thing. The rate of obesity in America had exploded.

Overweight for Life

Something else stood out in the survey. A lot of the weight gain was happening to kids. Before 1980, almost everyone followed the same path. Most teenagers were thin. Most adults added just a few pounds between the ages of twenty and forty. That's not true anymore.

Today more and more kids are overweight or obese. That means they weigh more when they become adults. Then they *keep* adding pounds as they get older. The average young person enters adulthood approximately 18 pounds heavier than just four decades ago.

We Didn't Change—Our Food Did

What had happened in such a short time to add so many millions of pounds to so many millions of people? I spent a long time researching this. The answer I came up with surprised me.

Something had changed in America, but it wasn't us. It was our food. Not just any food, but the kind of processed food made by big food companies.

I'm sure you've heard that junk food or fast food is bad for you. Maybe you've heard that it has too many calories, too much fat. You may know that fast food doesn't give you the right mix of proteins, fat, and and carbohydrates your body needs to be healthy. But there's one thing I bet you haven't heard before.

These kinds of foods make us fat because *they make us want to eat more.* These processed foods, loaded with sugar, fat, and salt, make it almost impossible for some people to stop eating.

Controlled by Cookies

Like Sarah, the woman I saw on television, millions of Americans are struggling with being overweight or obese. They know it's bad for them. They know it is making them very sick. And, like Sarah, eating so much makes them feel bad about themselves. Yet, also like Sarah, they *cannot stop eating.*

Some thin people have the same problem. They eat all the time. They cannot control themselves. When they see food, they just have to eat it.

After I saw Sarah on TV, I decided to perform an experiment. I walked into a bakery and asked for two chocolate-chip cookies. Back home, I pulled the cookies out of their bag and placed them on a paper plate. I put the plate just beyond my arm's reach. The cookies were thick and gooey—filled with chunks of chocolate.

The experiment began. I wanted to see if I could resist eating them. I sat and looked at the cookies. I sighed deeply and bit my lower lip. I found I was so focused on those cookies, I couldn't think of anything else. After a while, I noticed that I had moved my right hand a few inches closer to them. But I didn't intend to move my hand!

I tried reading the newspaper or thinking about something else. No matter what I did, I kept glancing back to the cookies. So I forced myself to head to my upstairs office, which is about as far away from the kitchen as I can get. But even from that safe distance, I could not fully shake the image of the cookies.

Finally, I left the house without having eaten those cookies. I felt I had won a big battle. But I hadn't, not really. Hours later, I went to a café I knew. A large glass jar filled with home-made cookies sat on the counter. I ordered an orange-chocolate cookie and ate it at once. Those cookies in my kitchen had won.

This was exactly the kind of behavior that made Sarah so unhappy. I just couldn't get those cookies out of my mind. Even though I knew I shouldn't eat them, I couldn't help myself. Like so many people, I felt I just could not control my urge to eat. I was determined to find out why.

CHAPTER 3

Eating and *Overeating*

People get fat because they eat too much. I know this seems obvious, but it's worth repeating.

Sometimes you hear other explanations. For example, you might hear that it all depends on the type of food you eat. Maybe it's carbohydrates, things like bread and pasta that are making us fat. Or you might hear that some people just naturally get fat because of their genes. Or maybe it's their metabolism—how fast they burn calories.

But after years of research and debate, scientists have proven that the simple explanation is the real one. If you eat more calories than your body needs, you will turn those extra calories into fat.

☞ **People gain weight because they eat more than their bodies need.**

In one important research project, scientists studied two groups of people. One group was gaining weight and the other was not. Over several months, the researchers recorded every single bite the two groups ate. To make sure they were counting every calorie, people in both groups had to take photographs of all their food.

The results of the study were very clear. The people who were gaining weight were eating about *400 calories more* every day. That equals a gain of about two pounds every two or three weeks.

In another study, scientists recorded the weight gain of a group of children for several years. They kept track of how much exercise the kids got. They compared the kids to their parents to see if they had inherited a weight problem. In the end, they discovered once again that the answer was simple. The children who ate more weighed more.

By the way, I want to be clear—exercise does help keep off the weight. That's because when you exercise you burn more calories. Plus exercise does all sorts of other great things for you—like keep you healthy and happy. But the simple fact remains, the main reason people gain weight is because they eat more than their bodies need.

• • • • • • • • • • • • • •

▶ **WHAT ARE CALORIES?** ◀

Your body burns foods to get energy. That energy is measured in calories. Carbohydrates, fats, sugars, and proteins all contain calories. When you eat more calories than your body needs, it stores the extra calories as fat.

• • • • • • • • • • • • • • • • • •

Out of Balance

Our bodies can balance themselves in many ways. For example, your body temperature is always about 98.6 degrees Fahrenheit. To make sure this happens, many parts of the body communicate with one another. Brain cells, nerve cells, skin, sweat glands, and blood vessels are all part of the network that keeps your temperature even.

You can see and feel this system at work every day. For instance, when you get too hot, you start to sweat. The evaporation of the sweat cools your skin and keeps your body temperature from rising.

In the same way, your body should balance the calories we consume (our energy intake) with the calories we burn (our energy use). How does this work? Very simply, when you need food, you get hungry. When you've had enough to eat, you feel full and stop eating. This energy balance system should keep our weight steady.

At least that's the way it's supposed to work. But something is throwing that system out of balance for many people. It turns out that certain kinds of foods can overpower this system. These are foods that do not exist in nature—foods that are loaded with lots of sugar, fat, and salt.

Food on the Brain

Your brain is very complex. It contains billions of nerve cells, and they are all doing different things. Only one small part of your brain is keeping track of energy balance. There are many other systems, all operating at once. Foods that taste good trigger a different part of your brain, the reward system.

The reward system in your brain, like the energy balance system, evolved over millions of years. They both help keep us alive. The energy balance system makes sure we get enough energy. The reward system makes sure we remember things that are good, things we will want to do again. The brain also keeps track of things that are bad or dangerous, to help us avoid them in the future.

From an energy perspective, we may not need any more food. We don't need that chocolate chip cookie for energy. But at the same time, the reward system may tell you that cookie is going to taste really good. It says you really, really have to eat that cookie.

In America, in the fight between energy balance and reward, the reward is winning.

☞ Foods loaded with sugar, fat, and salt activate
your brain's reward center.

▶ **DEFINITION: STIMULUS** ◀

In biology, a stimulus is something that causes a reaction in your body. (The plural of stimulus is *stimuli*.) We can say that good-tasting foods are stimuli. That means they activate, or *stimulate*, nerve cells in our brains. They *stimulate* the brain's reward system.

• • • • • • • • • • • • • • • •

Super-Stimuli

When it comes to the brain's reward system, not all foods are equal. An apple and a bowl of ice cream both taste good. But the ice cream is going to affect your brain differently than the apple. It triggers your reward system to make you want to eat even more. You might say the ice cream is a super-stimulus. Both taste good. Which one makes you want to eat more?

It's not just ice cream. Foods with large amounts of sugar, fat, and salt have a very powerful effect on your brain's reward system. Think of the cold, creamy pleasure of a milk shake, the aroma of chocolate cake, the texture of crispy chicken wings sweetened with a honey-mustard dipping sauce. Just thinking of them probably makes you feel like eating. A few seconds ago, you weren't even hungry. But if you're like most people, now you want to eat. Just the idea of those foods is enough to stimulate your brain's reward center.

Why are sugar, fat, and salt such powerful stimuli? Our ancestors *never* tasted the amount of sugar in a piece of chocolate cake or a candy bar. Their only source of sugar were natural sources like ripe fruit and honey. Their diets were also low in fat, perhaps no more than 10 percent of their food. So our bodies and our brains evolved in a world where sugar and fat were rare. When we taste something that is high in sugar and fat, our reward centers go into high gear. Our brains are wired to make sure we pay attention, so we can remember where to get this important high-energy food.

The problem is, in the modern world, sugar and fat are no longer rare. You can get them almost anywhere: in a supermarket, from a vending machine, in a drugstore, in a fast food restaurant. Some kids find them in their school cafeterias. Often all it takes is a walk to your refrigerator. We know that these foods are no longer scarce. But our brains are hardwired to tell us to eat as much of this stuff as we can get.

Two Stimuli Are Better Than One

We are born liking the taste of sugar. If you give something sweet to a baby, he or she will smile. Babies don't have to learn to like sugar, they just do. Sugar triggers the reward center in a baby's brain. But sugar by itself is not as powerful a stimulus as sugar mixed with fat.

Adam Drewnowski, at the University of Washington, in Seattle, has spent many years studying human taste and diet. At first he only studied how our bodies react to sugar. Soon he became convinced that it wasn't just the sugar in sweet foods that we liked. Fat, combined with sugar, makes a food so powerful it is hard for us to resist it.

Drewnowski conducted an experiment. He started with five different dairy products: skim milk, whole milk, half-and-half, heavy cream, and heavy cream blended with vegetable oil. Each one has a different percentage of fat. Skim milk has almost no fat while the cream-and-oil mixture was more than 50 percent fat.

He made mixtures of each liquid with different amounts of sugar. Then he asked people to taste them and tell him which one they liked best. The skim milk with sugar got low marks. It had lots of sugar but little fat. The unsweetened cream also didn't test too well. It had a lot of fat but no sugar. Which mixtures did people like the most? The ones with sugar *and* high fat content.

High Fat Rats

Barry Levin is a doctor and professor at the New Jersey Medical School. He performed an experiment with rats that proved the power of high-fat, high-sugar foods.

He began with two different types of rats. One group of rats always ate too much. If you fed them a high-calorie diet, they would keep eating until they became obese. The second type of rat did not usually eat too much. They stopped eating when they had enough. Then Levin offered both groups of rats a rich, creamy liquid high in sugar and fat. What happened? Both types of rats started overeating. Even the rats that didn't usually overeat could not resist a high-fat, high-sugar diet. They stuffed themselves and grew just as fat as the first group of rats.

Anthony Sclafani, when he was a graduate student at the University of Chicago, performed another experiment with rats. One group of rats ate only the regular rat chow pellets. He fed another group high-fat food. They gained more weight than the rats eating the chow, but not a lot more.

Then, by chance, he put a rat on a lab bench near some fallen Froot Loops, the high-calorie, high-sugar cereal. He was struck by how fast the animal picked up the cereal and started to eat it.

Sclafani decided to add Froot Loops to the experiment. First he let the rats taste the Froot Loops. Then he let them loose in an open space with some Froot Loops on the other side. Rats usually prefer to stay in corners and usually won't go across a field to eat chow pellets. But these rats didn't hesitate to run across the field to get the Froot Loops. The pull of the Froot Loops was so powerful, it made the rats ignore their natural fear of open spaces.

Next, Sclafani tested the rats with a "supermarket diet." The mix of foods he fed his animals could be purchased at any grocery store: sweetened condensed milk, chocolate-chip cookies, salami, cheese, bananas, marshmallows, milk chocolate, and peanut butter. After ten days, animals that were fed the supermarket diet weighed much more than rats that were fed rat chow. And the rats on the supermarket diet continued to gain weight, until they became twice as heavy as the rats eating chow.

Rats given chow stopped eating when they were full. Rats given high-fat, high-sugar food never stopped eating. Feeding rats a variety of processed foods from the supermarket turned out to be a very good way of making them obese.

People, Too

Experiments with humans also show the power of high-fat, high-sugar foods. In one experiment, a group of men were closely watched twenty-four hours a day. Everything they ate was recorded.

For the first few days, the men were fed a diet designed to keep them at their current body weight. They could not overeat because they weren't given extra calories. An average-weight adult male will need about 2,000 calories a day.

Then the men were allowed to eat whatever they wished from two free vending machines. The machines held a variety of foods including meats, cheese, and bread; tortillas and pinto beans; cereal, pastry, and desserts; french fries, popcorn, and chips; fruits, vegetables, nuts, and beverages.

You've probably guessed the result. Given the opportunity to eat whatever they wanted, the men ate an average of 4,500 calories daily. That's much more (150 percent more) than what they needed to maintain a stable weight. One person consumed almost 7,000 calories, the equivalent of about seventeen quarter-pound hamburgers. In general, the men also ate more fat and less protein.

So it turns out that people and rats have this in common: high-sugar, high-fat, high-salt foods will make most of us eat too much.

CHAPTER 4

Selling You Sugar, Fat, and Salt

Many years ago, the food industry managed to figure out that they could sell more food if it had a lot of sugar, fat, and salt in it. They didn't discover this through brain research. They just figured it out through trial and error. And once they figured it out, processed foods became the most important part of their business by far. In fact, you could say that the food industry is not really in the business of selling you food. They're in the business of delivering the taste of sugar, fat, and salt to your brain.

As a high-level food industry executive told me, "Higher sugar, fat, and salt make you want to eat more."

This executive agreed to show me how his industry operates. To protect his business, he did not want to be identified. He explained that the food industry creates dishes to hit what he called the "three points of the compass." That's right—sugar, fat, and salt.

☞ Food companies use sugar, fat, and salt to get you to buy their products.

Over the past twenty years, there has been an explosion in these kinds of processed foods. Today, Americans spend much of their food budget in restaurants. Many if not most of those restaurants are selling highly processed fast food or other food loaded with those three magic ingredients. Sugar, fat, and salt are sometimes loaded into the basic food (such as meat, vegetable, potato, or bread). Sometimes the magic three are layered on top. Deep-fried tortilla chips are an example of loading—the fat is contained in the chip itself. When a potato is smothered in cheese, sour cream, and sauce, that's layering.

I asked the food executive to describe the ingredients in some foods commonly found in popular restaurants today.

Potato skins: Usually the potato is hollowed out and the skin is fried. This provides more surface area for what he calls "fat pickup." Then some combination of bacon bits, sour cream, and cheese is added. The result is fat on fat on fat on fat, loaded with salt.

Cheese fries: "Take a high-fat food and put more fat on top of it," he said. The potato base is a simple car-bohydrate. That quickly breaks down to sugar in the body. Once it's fried and layered with cheese, we're eating salt on fat on fat on sugar.

Buffalo wings: Start with the fatty parts of a chicken, which get deep-fried. Then they're served with creamy or sweet dipping sauce that's heavily salted. Usually they're fried a first time at a production plant, then fried again at the restaurant, which essentially doubles the fat. That gives us sugar on salt on fat on fat on fat.

Spinach dip: There's not much spinach in it. The spinach provides little more than color and the idea that you're eating a vegetable. A high-fat, high-salt dairy product is the main ingredient. It's a tasty dish of salt on fat.

Chicken tenders: These are so loaded with batter and fat that my source jokes that they're a UFO—an unidentified fried object. Salt and sugar are loaded into the fat.

White Chocolate Mocha Frappuccino: Although Starbuck's stores were crowded early in the day, by afternoon they were fairly empty. Creating this "dessert in a cup" brought in crowds of customers later in the day. It's more like a milk shake than coffee, filled with a mix of sugar, fat, and salt. The whipped cream is optional.

Bloomin' Onion: This trademark Outback Steakhouse dish is very popular. Like a potato skin, the onion provides plenty of surface area to absorb fat. Fried in batter and topped with sauce, their flavor comes from salt on sugar on fat.

Salads: What's wrong with salads? They contain vegetables, of course, but in today's restaurants they're more than likely to be smothered in a high-fat cream-based ranch dressing and flavored with cheese chunks, bacon bits, and oily croutons. The food consultant calls this "fat with a little lettuce," although there's salt in the salad as well. Even lettuce has become a vehicle for fat.

A Recipe for Overeating

I began reading the Cheesecake Factory menu to my industry source. The restaurant chain is known for its vast spaces and equally vast portions.

We started with the appetizers.

Tex Mex Eggrolls: The menu said, "Spicy chicken, corn, black beans, peppers, onions, and melted cheese. Served with avocado cream and salsa." The food consultant said the avocado alone is about 15 to 20 percent fat, and that's before any mayonnaise or heavy cream is loaded in. A fried outer layer wraps fat and salt around more fat.

Roadside Sliders: "Bite-sized burgers on mini-buns served with grilled onions, pickles, and ketchup." The words suggest a cute, little hamburger. Inside it's the same thing: salt and fat in the meat, and sugar and salt in the onions and the ketchup. In reality, this dish is fat surrounded by layers of sugar on salt on sugar on salt, making it another grand slam.

Chicken Pot Stickers: "Oriental dumplings pan-fried in the classic tradition. Served with our soy dipping sauce." Frying the pot stickers loads them with fat. The layer of meat inside is loaded with salt, while the outside layer of sauce is loaded with sugar and salt. "That's hitting all the points," my source said.

Buffalo Blasts: "Chicken breast, cheese, and our spicy buffalo sauce, all stuffed in a spiced wrapper and fried until crisp. Served with celery sticks and blue cheese dressing."

For a moment the food consultant just laughed. "What can I say? That's fat, sugar, and salt." Chicken breast might make us think it is a low-fat dish. The celery sticks also hint at something healthy. But the cheese layer is at least 50 percent fat and carries a load of salt, and the buffalo sauce adds a layer of sugar on salt. That dough wrapper is fried and so absorbent that he called it "a fat bomb."

The "real" food in these dishes is just an excuse to deliver sugar, fat, and salt. Pizza crust is a way to deliver sugar and fat. Caesar salads are built as an excuse to carry fat and salt. We double-fry french fries, first at the factory and then in the restaurant. Our hamburgers are layered with bacon and cheese. We add cheese to spinach, batter our fish before frying it, and slather our Mexican food with cheese.

What the food industry is doing, my contact said, is using our minds and desires to make us buy their products.

CHAPTER 5

Why Diets Are Difficult

For years I wondered why I was fat. Science seemed to suggest there was nothing I could do about it.

Many doctors and scientists said that everyone had a natural set point for their weight. The idea is that your weight will naturally settle at a fixed point. If you try to lose weight by eating less, then your body will slow down its metabolism and use less energy. According to this theory, I was fat because my "set point" was high.

If it were true, this theory explained why so many people had trouble losing weight. It said if you dieted and ate less, your body would slow down to keep you from losing weight. It was almost a losing battle.

But if the set point theory were true, why did it only work when I tried to lose weight? It should also protect me from weight gain. When I eat more, my body should speed up my metabolism to burn more energy, but it does not.

My research has led me to a different conclusion. What is

the difference between people who can stay at a healthy weight and those who are overweight and obese? The answer, I believe, is that people have different responses to the foods high in sugar, fat, and salt that are all around us. If those types of foods have a strong pull on us, it is very hard not to gain weight and even harder to lose it.

☞ **Many people cannot resist foods that are loaded with sugar, fat, and salt.**

The Cookies Are Calling

To help me understand how different people react to food, I asked four friends to talk to me about food. My friend Claudia can't help thinking about frozen chocolate peanut-butter cookies. She calls them Charlie cookies, and they're one of her favorite desserts. In addition to chocolate chips and peanut butter, they contain oats, corn syrup, brown sugar, butter or margarine, vanilla, and salt. Basically, the oats are there to deliver three kinds of sweeteners, plus fat and salt, topped with a frosting of semisweet chocolate chips and peanut butter.

One day I spotted Claudia walking down the hallway with a plate of them, and I asked her to describe their appeal. "The chocolate smell is very distracting," she said. "I keep looking at them and thinking how good it would taste to have a bite. My stomach is starting to react. The back of my tongue tingles."

Claudia knows exactly what that first bite of frozen cookie

will taste like. She can describe it without even taking a bite. "It takes only a few chews for the chocolate-peanut butter layer to melt. As it does, the flavor goes from a cold spot on my tongue to very warm and mushy, a salty-sweet mush that seems to fill my entire mouth."

"The flavor is actually strongest after I've already swallowed the bite," she told me. "It just makes me want to eat more."

Maria is another friend. Like Claudia, she is overweight. Before we talked, I bought some of her favorite snacks, cake rolls. I put them on the table between us. (Maria knew I was going to do this—I wasn't playing a trick on her.)

"I just want to reach over, grab them, and take a bite," she sighed. As she talked, I could almost see her desire. Maria said she had not been thinking about food, and she hadn't felt hungry. But now she couldn't help staring at the cake. She imagined how it would feel and taste in her mouth. She knew she wouldn't be able to resist for long. "I keep looking at it," she admitted. "I'm fooling myself by thinking that I'll eat only one."

Suddenly Maria became angry. "I do not want them," she said. "But I cannot control my desire to eat them.

"I'm obsessing. I feel totally out of control."

A Constant Battle

The struggle that was taking place in Maria's brain is one that millions of Americans go through every day.

Claudia had the same problem. So do I. We argue with our-selves over eating something that seems really good to us. And we always lose the argument. Even though we feel we shouldn't eat it, we eat it anyway.

Rosalita is thin, but like Claudia and Maria, she spends a lot of time thinking about food. The day we talked, she told me she had already eaten some chocolate and had four cookies the previous evening.

I put some M&Ms on the table between us. Like Maria with the cake rolls, Rosalita had trouble resisting the M&Ms. "First I'll eat just a few, not a lot." she explained. "Then I'll have a few more. And I'll keep doing that until I feel sick."

Rosalita feels the same urge to eat as Maria and Claudia. She manages to stay thin with a lot of effort and struggle. When food is around, she thinks about it constantly. She told me when someone brings cookies into the office, "I'll eat one, go to my desk, and think about them. Then I'll go back for another one. And I'll do that for the rest of the afternoon."

However, not everyone feels the pull of high sugar, high fat foods. Like Rosalita, Jacob is thin. But he doesn't have to go through a constant struggle. For example, he likes M&Ms, but he doesn't need to eat them. When I offered him some, he looked at the bag and said, "I'm full. I already had a cookie about an hour and a half ago." He liked sweets, he explained, but had no desire to eat them when he wasn't hungry.

Jacob says he eats mostly for fuel. Food is just not that big a deal to him, and he rarely gives it much thought. "I just want to get eating out of the way," he says. When they heard this, Claudia and Maria couldn't understand his attitude.

Claudia, Maria, and Rosalita don't have an eating disorder. It's just that like many people, they feel powerless in the face of certain foods. How can M&Ms, Charlie cookies, and cake rolls have such control over us? Other foods don't have the same power. You never hear of someone who can't stop thinking about carrots or apples or green beans. What is it about these foods that make them different? I knew I had to find out.

CHAPTER 6

Food That Makes You Want More

Good food should make you feel full and satisfied. But we've seen that foods that are high in sugar, fat, and salt have the opposite effect on many people. Instead of easing our hunger and making us satisfied, these foods make us want to eat more. Even when we're full, even when we're *not hungry*, we feel we have to have more of these foods.

One way to describe this is that these foods are *reinforcing*. I put an M&M in my mouth, it tastes good, and right away I want another. The sugar and fat in the candy strengthen or *reinforce* my desire to keep eating it. Scientists have tested this and found it to be true.

To test if animals find a food or drug reinforcing, scientists try to answer two questions: First, are the animals willing to work to get it? How many times will they press a lever or perform some other task to get the food? Second, will they respond the same way to some other signal they connect with the food? For example, if you ring a bell every time they get the food, will the animals begin to respond to the bell the way they respond to the food?

If you perform these experiments with foods high in sugar, fat, and salt, you discover they are clearly reinforcing.

☞ Foods loaded with sugar, fat, and salt are reinforcing. They make many people want to eat more.

Not Hungry? Eat Anyway

One experiment scientists have performed is simple. French researchers divided lab animals into two groups. One group could eat as much as they wanted. The other group was kept on a strict diet, to make sure they were hungry.

Next they gave each group a chance to get two types of food: regular chow and Choc and Crisp, a chocolate-flavored cereal high in sugar and fat. The scientists measured how fast the animals ran to the chow, and then separately, how fast they ran to the Choc and Crisp.

The hungry rats ran faster toward the chow than the rats that were not hungry. But both groups, the hungry animals and the ones that were not hungry, ran toward the Choc and Crisp cereal at almost the same speed. Let me repeat that: Animals that *were not hungry* ran to get the high-sugar, high-fat food. The experiment proves these foods are reinforcing. Animals will work for them even if they're not hungry. This has been proven many times.

Another experiment, at Carleton University in Ottawa, Ontario, forced rats to work harder and harder to get their next reward. At the beginning, getting a reward was easy. When an animal pressed a lever once, it earned a reward. However to get the second reward, the rat had to press the lever three times. The next one took six presses. A fourth reward took ten lever presses, a fifth took sixteen, and a sixth took twenty-three presses of the lever.

In an experiment like this, researchers look for the breaking point. They want to see if there is a point beyond which the animal will not keep pressing. Sure enough, the rats worked harder to get sugar. They also worked harder for higher amounts of sugar. On average, the rats pressed the lever enough times to get six rewards of a 10 percent sucrose solution and eight rewards of a 20 percent sucrose solution. To get that eighth reward of 20 percent solution, the rats had to press the lever forty-four times. The sweeter the sugar solution, the longer they would work until they gave up.

Tests also show that lab animals prefer mixtures of sugar and fat. Sara Ward, a researcher at the University of North Carolina at Chapel Hill, tested mice to see if they would work to get a drink called Ensure. Ensure is marketed as being a "healthy" protein drink, but it is high in sugar and fat.

To get a drink of Ensure, the mice had to poke their noses

through a hole. Just like the rats working for sugar, the mice had to work harder for each new drink. The mice were ready to work very hard for Ensure. On average, they didn't stop until they had gotten fourteen rewards. Remember, each reward required more nose pokes than the one before. To get the fourteenth reward took *seventy-seven* nose pokes.

Ward told me that the power of sugar and fat was only slightly less than cocaine, a highly addictive drug. Animals will work almost as hard to get either one. When a food is almost as powerful as cocaine, we know it is highly reinforcing.

Food Cues

The second test for reinforcement is whether animals will respond to signals, or cues, they connect with the food. For example, if animals always get the food in the same spot, then when they are placed in that spot they will begin wanting the food—whether the food is there or not. These cues can become as powerful as the food itself. They take over our thoughts and attention, and they make us feel the urge we call "wanting."

A bowl of M&Ms, for example, can be reinforcing before I touch a single one. If I've eaten the candy in the past, I know it will be rewarding. Just the sight of it can make me reach for an M&M, eat it, and experience that reward.

Of course, once I've eaten the M&M, and had that feeling of pleasure, the sight of M&Ms will be an even stronger cue for me. I can get trapped in a cycle. I see the cue, I want the food, I eat it, and then the cue becomes even more powerful. That's how eating habits develop.

In one experiment, rats could move between two identical cages. Scientists measured how much time the rats spent in each cage. There was no food in either one and the animals were not hungry. Usually the rats spent more time in one cage. They seemed to prefer it.

In the second part of the test, the researchers divided the rats into two groups. Each group got regular rat chow in the cage they liked most. In the second cage, the one the rats hadn't preferred, one group got Froot Loops and the other group got Cheetos. You can guess what happened. The rats spent more time in the cages they hadn't liked because now the cages contained high-sugar, high-fat treats.

But that wasn't the end of the experiment. The researchers repeated the test, this time with no food in either cage. But the rats didn't go back to their old ways. They spent more time in the cages where they had come to expect the high-calorie treats. In their brains, the cages had become connected with the treats.

For humans, too, location is one of the most powerful cues. Pass the mall where you know you'll find a favorite restaurant or drive down a street where you know there is great pizza. What happens? You'll experience desire you didn't have a moment before. You associate a place with a certain food, and just being in that place makes you want to eat.

CHAPTER 7

Training Your Brain

How exactly does food affect the brain? The most important way we experience food is with our sense of taste. The sight and smell of food, the feel of food in our mouths can all add to the pleasure of eating, but taste is the most important factor.

When we taste something, nerve cells on our tongue react to the food. (Nerve cells are called *neurons*.) These are the cells of our taste buds. The brain is made up of many different types of neurons. Neurons also carry electrical signals back and forth between the brain and the rest of the body.

Neurons in our taste buds react when they come in contact with food. They fire electrical signals, which travel along neurons to the brain. Another way of saying this is that the neuron is *stimulated* by the food. It reacts to *stimuli* by sending an electrical signal to the brain. The stronger the stimuli, the more the neurons will fire.

Some neurons respond to only a single type of food or taste. For example, some neurons will react to sweetness. Others will react to salt. Some neurons react to a combination of tastes. And, as you might guess, there are neurons that can detect the presence of sweet, fatty foods. For example, a neuron stimulated by a sweet taste and a fatty texture would be active when we eat a piece of chocolate cake loaded with sugar, fat, and salt.

When the taste buds in your mouth come into contact with foods loaded with sugar, fat, and salt, a stream of signals is sent to the brain. Those signals go straight to the part of the brain that responds to pleasure. Taste is directly wired into the reward center of your brain. That is one reason taste is so powerful and can create strong emotions.

☞ Eating high-sugar, high-fat foods has
a powerful effect on your brain.

Feel-Good Food

When we eat something that tastes good, neurons in the brain release chemicals known as *endorphins*, or *opioids*. These chemicals make us feel pleasure. (Some drugs, including heroin and morphine, have the same effect on your brain as opioids.) Super-sweet, super-fatty foods make those neurons fire more and release even more opioids. We feel even more pleasure.

Opioids not only make us feel pleasure, they relieve pain. They relieve stress and make us feel calmer. That's why eating high-sugar, high-fat foods makes us feel better—at least in the short run. This sets off another cycle. Eating these food releases opioids in our brain. This increases our enjoyment of the food. The feeling of pleasure makes us want to eat more of the same food, which releases more opioids and so on.

Experiments on animals have shown the link between brain chemistry and eating foods loaded with sugar, fat, and salt. If you give animals an injection of opioids, they will eat more high-sugar, high-fat food. If you give them a drug that blocks the production of opioids, they will eat less high-sugar, high-fat food.

Opioids can also change our desire for foods. Many animals, including humans, naturally crave variety in food. This means that after we eat a lot of one food, we get tired of it and want something different. But when these high-sugar, high-fat foods create a lot of opioid activity in the brain, this changes.

When a food stimulates a lot of opioid production in our brains, we don't grow tired of it. The opioids change our natural desire for variety. We just want more of the same opioid-producing food. The reverse is also true. If we block the production of opioids in the brain, animals will eat less of the high-sugar, high-fat foods. Without opioids, the food cannot create the same feeling of pleasure in the brain.

Pay Attention to This!

Once you understand the role of opioids, you can understand why foods loaded with sugar, fat, and salt are so hard to resist. They work on our brain chemistry in the same way that some drugs do. And that's only half the story. Foods that are loaded with sugar, fat, and salt also stimulate your brain to create another chemical, called *dopamine*. Dopamine production is another reason that these foods make us want to eat more.

Opioids give food its pleasure. Dopamine works differently. Dopamine is like a bright flashing light in your brain that says, "Here is something important." When a stimulus creates dopamine in the brain, we pay careful attention, so we can remember what it is and then get more of it.

Dopamine is important for survival. It helps us focus on things we need. It gives us the drive to get things that are good for us. When something gives us pleasure, like food, then the brain produces dopamine. The dopamine focuses our attention on the food, and it makes us work hard to get it. The more rewarding the food, the more we will focus on getting it. For example, lab rats won't work hard to get food if their dopamine levels are kept low.

Drugs like cocaine and amphetamines work on our brains by increasing our dopamine levels. Foods that are high in sugar, fat, and salt aren't drugs, but they do raise our dopamine levels.

The two types of brain chemicals, opioids and dopamine, work together. When we eat a high-sugar, high-fat food, opioids make us feel pleasure. Dopamine makes us pay attention and drives us to want more. These two are part of the reward system in your brain They are a big part of why your reward system drives you to seek out more high-sugar, high-fat foods.

More Is Better

Here's another fact of biology that makes it hard to resist high-sugar, high-fat foods: Our brains are wired to make us feel that *more* is better. If one food is sweeter than another, it will make our brains release more dopamine. That makes us focus on the sweeter food and want it more. If we naturally like a certain food, such as sweets, then we will like super-sweet food even more.

For millions of years, as human beings evolved, there was no danger in this. Our brains pushed us to find more sweet and fatty foods, because most of the time we could never get enough. Today's super-sweet, super-fatty foods just didn't exist, so there was no danger we would overeat. Now, when we taste these foods, our brains tell us to keep eating, as though these foods were still scarce.

That's also why restaurant chains serve such huge portions. We don't need those huge super-sized portions to satisfy our hunger. But seeing large amounts of food stimulates our desire to eat. It's hardwired into our brains that more is better. Give people two scoops of ice cream and chances are they'll eat all of it, even if they were only hungry enough for one.

Of course, in the modern world, super-sweet, super-fatty foods are all over the place. But we have no built-in defense against them. We have to retrain our brains so we will no longer be driven to overeat.

CHAPTER 8

The Food Carnival

Besides loading our food with sugar, fat, and salt, what other tricks does the food industry use? One trick is to attack our taste buds with lots of combinations of flavors and textures. I understand this on a very personal level. It's one reason I find it hard to resist chocolate frozen yogurt with sprinkles and cookie dough.

When I was a kid, it was a special treat to get a store-bought ice-cream cone. The flavors were pretty simple: vanilla, chocolate, and strawberry, with maybe coffee or one or two others. Over time, many more flavors became available.

In the 1970s, Steve's Ice Cream was the most famous ice-cream parlor in the Boston area. People loved to go there and ask for "smoosh-ins"—Heath bars, Reese's peanut butter cups, and other confections—mixed into a scoop of ice cream. These added flavors and textures (not to mention the added fat) made the ice cream more desirable.

Today, chains like Cold Stone Creamery and 16 Handles have taken that model to a new level. At 16 Handles, you start by picking a flavor of frozen yogurt. You can even pick a nonfat yogurt if you want to feel healthy. But then you add toppings—fruit, yes, but also cookies, chocolate chips, gummy bears, chocolate syrup, and more. Cold Stone Creamery does the same thing with ice cream. These chains are popular hangouts, where mixing and eating high-sugar, high-fat food becomes a pastime.

The food industry has figured out that by combining different flavors, it could make foods that were even harder for most people to resist. They applied this lesson to all sorts of foods, not just ice cream and frozen yogurt. For example, not long ago, there were just a few kinds of bagels—plain, sesame, or poppy seeds. Now bagels come flavored with onions, garlic, cinnamon and raisins, blueberries, and chocolate.

☞ **The food industry uses many tricks to make us want to eat more.**

Loaded and Layered

The Panera Bread chain goes further, offering the cherry vanilla bagel, the French toast bagel, and the Dutch apple and raisin bagel. Each one comes loaded with sugar on fat on salt. My son says that Panera's cinnamon crunch bagel is the best he's ever eaten. It's the restaurant's top seller, so that's what I decided to try.

Taking my first bite, I concentrated on the number of different tastes in my mouth. The topping gave the bagel a crunchy sweetness, which contrasts nicely with the soft inside. The aroma of cinnamon was pleasantly strong, and the vanilla chips offered appealing bursts of flavor.

As I chewed, the bagel was quickly transformed into a moist mass in my mouth. It was easy to chew and to swallow, and its sweetness lingered yet didn't overwhelm the other flavors. Helped by the high-fat content, the bagel melted perfectly in my mouth, disappearing after only a few chews. The cinnamon crunch bagel was manufactured to perfection. Panera had figured out how to put fat, sugar, and other flavors together to provide exactly the sensory experience I wanted.

I call these types of foods "loaded and layered." They are loaded with huge amounts of sugar, fat, and salt. They are layered with many flavors, one on top of another. Everywhere you look, you will see processed foods made with this same principle—they are loaded and layered to get you hooked and get you to come back again and again.

The Food Industry Wants to Get Hold of You

This is the text of an ad for T.G.I. Friday's. It's a great example of how the restaurant chain promises you more than good food. They promise you a food carnival, with dozens of new and exciting stimuli. Also notice how they promise to "get hold of your appetite and not let go."

☞ This isn't about grabbing a bite. It's about a bite grabbing you. 'Cause when Friday's gets hold of your appetite, we're not letting go. We are going to bring on the flavor 'til your taste buds explode like fireworks. We are going to dribble glazes and pour on smoky sauces. We are going to pan-fry, sauté, and dream up new dishes that have never been created before. Three courses. New tastes.

Not enough? Just read this description of one appetizer from the menu, the Parmesan-Crusted Sicilian Quesadilla: "Packed with sautéed chicken, sausage, bruschetta marinara, bacon and oozing with Monterey Jack cheese. We coat it with Parmesan and pan-fry it to a crispy, golden brown, then drizzle it with balsamic glaze."

Whoever is designing the food at T.G.I.Friday's understands that food with lots of tastes is more powerful than simple food. Instead of one stimulus, the food delivers several at once. This increases our desire to have those foods again.

Pavlov's Dogs

As I've already explained, just seeing a place where we've enjoyed food can make us hungry. How does this work?

You may know the story of Russian scientist Ivan Pavlov and his dogs. In one famous experiment, Pavlov rang a bell every time he fed his dogs. After a while, the dogs began to salivate and drool at the sound of the bell, even if there was no food in sight. Their brains connected the sound of the bell with food. Or you could say they were conditioned to react to the bell the way they reacted to food.

People can be conditioned, too. You can be conditioned to respond to a time of day or an activity or golden arches that remind you of McDonald's. In one study, people were given a high-sugar, high-fat snack five mornings in a row. That was not their usual time to eat. But after just five days, they became conditioned to expect a snack at that time. For days after the experiment, they wanted something sweet at the same time each morning. They had the same response as if they saw or smelled the food—but the food wasn't there.

That's what happens when you become conditioned in this way. Your brain substitutes one stimulus for another. The dopamine in your brain is activated, just as if you were eating the food. If you see a package of snack food and you suddenly want to eat, it's a sign you have become conditioned to connect that packaging with the food.

Food companies understand this. Through marketing and advertising, they give us lots of signals and cues we connect with the good experience of eating their sugar, fat, and salt. A cue could be an advertisement on TV, or the picture from the package. When you see or hear the cue, you start wanting the food, sometimes without even knowing why. If you look at a Chihuahua and get hungry, don't worry. You've just been conditioned to think of Taco Bell whenever you see that little dog.

Memories Sell Food

To sell us more sugar, fat, and salt, food companies play on our emotions, too.

A reporter named Andrew told me this story: When he was a young boy in New York, he went to Carvel, the legendary ice-cream chain, to celebrate every Little League victory. The childhood memory still has power over him. Whenever he goes back to New York, he feels a great desire to head to Carvel. He has to fight not to give in. Food memories like these are yet another cue that turns on the brain's reward center. We may not even be aware of what is causing the desire.

One clear weekend afternoon, I drove across the Golden Gate Bridge with a friend named Bill. We were on a quest for a restaurant where he had eaten a special dessert—fifteen years before. The dessert was a strawberry milk shake inside a chocolate bag. (The bag was made by filling a paper bag with chocolate, then freezing it.)

It wasn't just the milk shake he remembered. He clearly remembered the day and the friends he was with. He had just finished traveling across the country and was about to get married. All those happy memories were linked in his mind with the milk shake. The problem was Bill couldn't remember the restaurant where he'd had it. But he couldn't get the memory of the food out of his mind. The memory was creating a very strong desire. We went from restaurant to restaurant searching for the special milk shake.

There is a strong connection among memory, emotion, and food. The food industry plays on this in its advertising. Often they aren't selling food directly—they are selling emotions. That's what the Applebee's campaigns "Eatin' Good in the Neighborhood" and "The Flavors That Bring People Together" are all about. The aim of these ads is to trigger a memory of a time you were happy with your friend or family. If they can get you to associate that good feeling with Applebee's, then you will feel a desire to eat there.

Once you understand this, you begin to look at food commercials differently. That fun, zippy Coke commercial isn't really selling you soda. It's getting you to connect the emotion of happiness with the act of drinking Coke. It might trigger a memory of a time when you were happy. You might even remember a time when you were happy while you were drinking Coke.

Once the food company can trigger the emotion, you will feel the desire to drink Coca-Cola or eat at Taco Bell. The food begins to have power over you. As the people from T.G.I. Friday's say, "This isn't about grabbing a bite. It's about a bite grabbing you."

CHAPTER 9

Sugar, Fat, and Salt Rewire Your Brain

As we've seen, your brain evolved to make you seek out rewards. The reward center in the brain releases dopamine to give you the drive to find the reward. This is important for survival. When our ancestors needed food, their brains urged them to keep looking until they found it.

But it is also important for survival to be able to *stop* looking for food. When you have found the food or other reward, the dopamine level in your brain should drop. Otherwise, you'd always be running around, using up energy for no reason. And that is exactly how the brain works—most of the time. Something triggers your brain to seek a reward, your brain releases dopamine, you find the reward, and the dopamine goes back down. It's yet another way the brain naturally seeks a balance.

But there are some things that can throw off the natural balance of the brain reward system. Some drugs, like cocaine, do this. Cocaine stimulates the brain so that you never stop wanting it. You are stimulated to seek out the next reward. That is why it is so addictive.

It turns out that certain kinds of foods act on the brain in the same way. They never stop stimulating the brain so you never stop wanting them. You are always driven to seek them out. What kinds of foods are these? I'm sure you have guessed by now. They are the foods super-loaded with sugar, fat, and salt.

> ☞ Foods loaded with sugar, fat, and salt
> change the chemistry of your brain.

Can't Get Enough

When lab rats are fed a high-sugar, high-fat chocolate drink, their dopamine goes up and stays up. They never get used to it (or *habituated*, to use the scientific term). Whenever the food is available, they will feel the desire to eat it. Whenever they can, they will work to get it.

Sadly, what is true for animals is true for humans. High-sugar, high-fat foods have the same effect on our brains (at least for most of us). This is one of the most important facts about foods loaded with sugar, fat, and salt—they don't work on our brains the way other foods do. We never get habituated to them. Once we have tasted them, we will almost always feel the desire to eat them if we can. A simple cue, or signal, will make us feel hungry, even if we are already full.

Once people fall into this cycle, the behavior becomes a habit. New pathways are built up in the brain. The response to cues and signals becomes almost automatic. And the more we follow the habit, *the stronger it becomes*.

This is the trap for people like Sarah, Claudia, Maria, and millions of others who feel they cannot control their response to food. It's not that they lack "willpower" or are weak. The sugar, fat, and salt are working on their brain chemistry in a way that is almost irresistible. The foods are rewiring their brains.

Eating Without Thinking

Say I walk into my house and decide to have ice cream. I will go to the refrigerator and take a carton from the freezer. I'll scoop out some ice cream, and I will eat it. I like to think that all of that activity is *my* choice. I have thought about it (even if it's just for a second) and made a decision to eat ice cream. Then I do what it takes to get the ice cream.

Now imagine another situation. I walk into my house and, *without thinking about it*, I go straight to the freezer, take out some ice cream, and start eating. I don't mean I am sleepwalking or in a trance. Rather, eating ice cream has become such a habit, I no longer make a decision to do it. Some part of my brain is working on it, but I am not conscious of it.

It's like when you walk home from school. Once you have done it a few times, you no longer have to think about it. You may even daydream while you walk and "snap out of it" at your front door without remembering how you got there.

Millions of people are eating this way. It's not because they are weak or have no self-control. Their brain patterns have been changed by something very powerful—foods loaded with sugar, fat, and salt. The more rewarding the food, the stronger the experience that creates the automatic behavior.

Habits are learned slowly, but once they are in place, they are very difficult to break. That's because they change the patterns of our brains. But there's a flip side to this. Just as we learn bad habits—habits that are harmful to us, like overeating—we can also learn new habits. Those new habits can lead us to a healthy, happier way of dealing with food, one where *we* are in control.

PART TWO

HOW THE FOOD INDUSTRY
TARGETS YOU

CHAPTER 10

A Visit to Chili's

Through years of research, I had learned how sugar, fat, and salt act on our brains. I'd learned that foods loaded with sugar, fat, and salt were in some ways like addictive drugs. I'd seen how these foods worked on our memories and emotions, how they made us want to eat more. And I'd met enough people like Claudia and Maria to understand how these foods could cause people to lose control.

But I wasn't the only one doing research. Big food companies have been working on the same problem for years. Only they haven't been trying to help people get control of their eating. They were figuring out ways to make foods like Monster Thickburgers and Baked! Cheetos Flamin' Hot. They were using research to make foods that people could *not* stop eating.

And they've been very successful.

One evening, I was sitting at Chili's Grill & Bar in Chicago's O'Hare Airport. I was waiting for a late-night flight. At a nearby table, I saw a man and a woman who were deep into a meal. The woman was overweight. I guessed she was five foot four inches and weighed about 180 pounds.

She was eating a dish called Southwestern Eggrolls. On the menu they were listed as a starter course. In spite of that, the huge platter was heaped with enough food for an entire meal. I watched as the woman attacked her food. She held an egg roll in one hand, dunked it into the sauce, and brought it to her mouth. Meanwhile she used the fork in her other hand to scoop up more sauce. Every few seconds she reached over and speared some of the man's French fries. She ate quickly, working her way around the plate without stopping. When she finally paused, only a little lettuce was left.

As I watched her eat, I wondered if she knew what she was eating. She probably didn't realize how the food was making her overeat. Then I wondered if *I* knew what she was eating. What was really in those egg rolls and all the other dishes on the menu? I decided to investigate, so I visited about twelve different Chili's. Often the places were full, and sometimes there were lines at the front door.

☞ **Processed foods are loaded with sugar,
fat, and salt.**

No-Chew Food

I asked a food industry expert to tell me about the Southwestern Eggrolls. He started with the tortilla. He explained that deep-frying the tortilla makes it absorb a lot of fat. Then he looked at the other ingredients. Salt appeared eight times on the label. Sweeteners were listed five times as corn syrup, molasses, honey, brown sugar, and sugar.

"There's green stuff in there," he said, noting the spinach. "That makes me feel like I'm eating something healthy. Then there's the cheese. The amount of cheese Americans eat is off the chart." The hot peppers, he said, "add a little spice, but not too much to kill everything else off."

He believed the chicken had been chopped and formed much like a meat loaf. Other ingredients were added to make the chicken soft. Some ingredients called "binders," hold it all together and add water. This is all done to make those calories easy to swallow.

"All of this has been processed so you can wolf it down fast," he explained.

By getting rid of the need to chew, processed food allows us to eat faster. "When you're eating these things, you've had 500, 600, 800, 900 calories before you know it," said the consultant. That's really true—you just don't know how much you're eating. The food simply melts in your mouth.

Packed with Fat

At one Chili's, a friend and I ordered Kickin' Jack Nachos, an appetizer, and two main dishes—Boneless Shanghai Wings and Margarita Grilled Chicken.

The Kickin' Jack Nachos chips were covered with a layer of mashed black beans and cheese. The Boneless Shanghai Wings were crispy breaded chicken served in a thick, sweet and spicy sauce. The Margarita Grilled Chicken was a grilled chicken breast served with rice, black beans, strips of fried tortilla, and salsa.

Out of the three dishes, my friend thought the Grilled Chicken was the most healthy. You might think so, too. But that's because you don't know how it is made. At the factory, the uncooked chicken had been soaked in a liquid that included sugar, two kinds of oil, and salt. Then it was frozen and shipped to the restaurant in twenty-five-pound bags, each containing about fifty pieces of meat.

Nick Nickelson is a scientist at a company that sells meat to Chili's. He told me that the chicken and sauce were tumbled together in a piece of equipment that resembled a cement mixer. This pulls the liquid into the meat, making it tender and easier to chew. Another common method is to shoot the sauce into the meat with hundreds of needles. This tears the meat, basically making it "pre-chewed."

They Don't Want You To Know

Every time I ordered food at a Chili's, I asked the server, "What's in this?" Sometimes I asked the same question of the manager. Strangely, the staff at Chili's couldn't answer my question.

"We can't tell you," one manager said flatly.

"I'm not sure I'm allowed to say," someone else told me.

Chili's probably doesn't want you to know that the chicken wings they serve have been pumped full of water, hydrolyzed soy protein, salt, and sodium phosphate. The water is to bulk up the chicken to make it seem like you're getting more. Also, water makes food softer and easier to chew.

At the factory, the chicken is also battered, breaded, and frozen. This creates a salty coating that becomes crispy when fried in fat. After it's cooked, the crispy coating is probably 40 percent fat. That fried batter is about half the volume of the nuggets on the plate. Then the chicken is served with a ginger-citrus sauce that is mainly sugar with a lot of salt. My food industry contact said it was "Sugar on sugar, really just different sugars. And lots of salt. And lots of intense flavor."

But wait, there's more! The fried and sweetened chicken is also served with a wasabi ranch dressing, which is made from mayonnaise, buttermilk, and spices. The wings are served in a basket lined with waxed paper and bits of strange-looking crispy noodles that absorb excess fat. The whole thing is designed to cram as much sugar, fat, and salt into one meal that can be eaten with as little chewing as possible.

CHAPTER 11

Cinnabon: Food You Can't Resist!

The Cinnabon story began in a farmhouse thirty-five miles outside Seattle, Washington. Every Sunday, family and friends gathered for legendary dinners of fried chicken, baked beans, and cinnamon rolls. Jerilyn Brusseau fondly remembers those dinners at her grandmother's house. She remembered the love her grandmother poured into those cinnamon rolls and the eager delight of the guests who ate them.

Brusseau grew up to be a cook herself and opened her own French-style bakery and café. She hadn't planned on serving her grandmother's country-style cinnamon rolls, but her family insisted. The café quickly became famous for the cinnamon rolls. People traveled great distances to try them. The *New York Times* even wrote about them.

And then, one day in 1985, the phone rang. Rich Komen was on the line. Komen is the founder of Restaurants Unlimited. As you might guess, the company owns restaurants.

"Jerilyn, I have an idea," Komen said. "How would you like to make the world's greatest cinnamon rolls?"

"You bet," Brusseau replied.

Together, the two started Cinnabon. Today, the chain seems to be in every mall and airport in America.

☞ **The food industry designs foods that are hard to resist.**

Making The Perfect Roll

Brusseau and Komen worked on every detail of the Cinnabon cinnamon roll. "We started from the outside in," says Brusseau. "We wanted it to look this certain way. We wanted it to be full and round and have many, many, many wraps." They also wanted it to have a certain smell. They wanted it to be so appealing that people couldn't resist it.

"We wanted a dough that had a quality like a pillow, a dough that would be soft," she remembers. "And then the syrup—the cinnamon caramel in the center would be very soft and syrupy so there would be this contrast of textures." They also wanted a creamy topping. "We wanted this creaminess . . . a cream that would actually be spooned over the top of the rolls." Their goal was a very rich, very enjoyable experience. Just the description of the Cinnabon gets my mouth watering. That's a cue.

For months, the partners baked and tested hundreds of cinnamon rolls. On top of everything else, they had to design rolls that could be cooked in stores across America and served warm within thirty minutes. They finally succeeded in their quest to develop a roll they thought was "absolutely irresistible." They must have been right. Cinnabon celebrated its twenty-fifth anniversary in 2010. It now has hundreds of stores worldwide.

What Makes the Yum?

I wanted to find out what went into "the world's greatest cinnamon rolls." What makes them so hard to resist? Brusseau told me the secret wasn't just the list of ingredients. It's the way everything is combined to make sure every single part of the roll is appealing. That includes the way it looks, smells, tastes, and feels in your mouth.

"The taste is so fulfilling," she explained. "It just has something that is yum." The cinnamon is very important, she said, because it creates emotions when you smell it. Something about it gives the eater a feeling of warmth and happiness.

I pushed her to talk about the ingredients. I knew that wheat and yeast were the starting points.

"Salt brings up the flavor," she told me.

"What's next?"

"Sugar." She explained why three different kinds are used. One type of sugar sweetens the dough and helps create its soft texture. A second kind is used in the sticky filling. Then powdered sugar is used in the frosting.

Brusseau said fat was added to make the roll tender and

rich. Cream cheese, which also has a lot of fat, is added to the frosting to give it "that really nice, creamy texture." The frosting helps create the special aroma that draws people in.

Serving the rolls warm is another important part of the experience. "Temperature creates this appeal. It heightens the aroma, it heightens the flavor, it heightens the whole sensory experience."

The Cinnabon people have thought of everything, including how the roll feels in your mouth when you eat it. First, you get a strong taste of cinnamon mixed with other flavors. Then you feel the soft dough and taste the creamy frosting.

Like the food at Chili's, the Cinnabon roll is made to go down with little chewing.

"It melts in your mouth. It disappears easily. The swallow is very nice," Brusseau said. "It's amazing to me how much people love Cinnabon."

The Fat "Mouthfeel"

The food industry has made up a word for the way food feels in your mouth. They call it "mouthfeel." They devote a lot of time, money, and energy to find the right mouthfeel for their products. Like the Cinnabon roll, a food with good mouthfeel combines several different tastes and textures. Then it melts away when you eat it.

Food industry experts spend years to get the perfect mouthfeel into processed food. One of these experts is Gail Civille. As president of Sensory Spectrum, a food industry consulting business, Civille probably knows as much as anyone in America about what consumers like to eat and why. She told me that to design irresistible food, you have to plan out every moment, from before the food enters the mouth until after it is eaten.

She told me that fat is very important because it makes food feel thicker and richer. Fat also helps release other flavors. In fact, some fats help release the flavor of other fats. That's why companies add butter to cheese. The butter helps the cheese flavor spread through your mouth.

Fat also helps food go down much more easily. When you chew something with added fat, it forms a nice chewy mass in your mouth. Then it melts away easily. People find this much more pleasant than chewing something hard that might leave bits of food stuck in their teeth. To eat a regular home-cooked meal, you might chew every bite twenty-five times. But processed food takes about ten chews per mouthful.

Different flavors mixed together boost your desire for the food. That's why some people like foods that are sweet and salty or spicy and sour. When we bite into cheese-covered fries with bacon, we are getting different flavors one after the other. Each flavor works on our reward system and makes us want more.

This is one way we get hooked on processed foods. We don't eat because we're hungry. We eat because we like the feel of the food in our mouth. We like the way the flavors mix together, the way it all goes down so easily. We are eating to get the right "mouthfeel." But that only lasts for a short time. The only way to get that mouthfeel again is to eat more.

Too Much of a Good Thing

The Cinnabon roll is a perfect example of a high-sugar, high-fat food that makes people want to eat more. It has made Jerilyn Brusseau rich. So I was a little surprised to hear her talk about the problem of childhood obesity. Brusseau is proud of her rolls and her success. But she understands the danger of overeating.

"I make cinnamon rolls for my family for special events. I make Cinnabons for friends. I love to teach people about the lineage of cinnamon rolls, about this ordinary food made extraordinarily well so that you can have a wonderful sensory experience. But I don't teach them to eat it four times a day. It's all a matter of balance.

"If someone today asked me to create the world's greatest cinnamon roll, I'd probably think differently about it," she told me. "Twenty years ago, it was a once-in-a-while treat. I wasn't so worried about obesity among kids. Now I am. . . . I'm very concerned that kids are growing up eating too many things like Cinnabon every day of their lives."

Brusseau knows about losing balance and being out of control with food. As a young woman, she battled eating disorders, including bulimia. As a chef and restaurant owner, she worked with food all day, but she could no longer tell when she was hungry and when she was full.

One way or another, millions of Americans have the same problem. Some of them are eating way too many Cinnabons.

CHAPTER 12

Food As Entertainment

Pink's is a hot dog stand. It has been on the same corner in Los Angeles since it started as a pushcart over sixty-five years ago. The food is legendary. On the walls are photographs of dozens of famous stars who've eaten there.

Today, Pink's sells more than plain old hot dogs. Among the twenty-one varieties available at Pink's are the Bacon Chili Cheese Dog, the Brooklyn Pastrami Swiss Cheese Dog, and the Three Dog Night Dog (three hot dogs wrapped in a giant tortilla and served with bacon, cheese, chili, and onions).

Gloria Pink, one of the owners, explained why plain hot dogs are no longer enough. "It's all about entertaining people," she said. "That's what the food business has become." Entertaining people with food means offering lots of different choices with extra add-ons.

Food as entertainment? I hadn't quite thought in those terms. Later I learned that the food industry had made up a word for this. They call it "eatertainment."

☞ If you think of food as "fun" or "entertainment,"
you'll forget about the calories.

Fat or Fun?

If food companies can sell food as entertainment, they can sell more of it. After all, you only need a certain amount of food every day. But there is no limit to the amount of entertainment you can consume. That's one reason the restaurant business sells over $300 *billion* worth of food a year.

Have you ever noticed the photos on the walls of fast food restaurants? You might be in a pizza place and there will be a color photograph of a cheese-and-pepperoni pizza on the wall. The photo is a cue to make you want more pizza. It promises you pleasure and fun if you eat. If you focus on the photo and the enjoyment, you will forget that you're already full, that you don't really need that third slice.

In the same way, food companies get you to focus on new types of foods with lots of added flavors and ingredients. Think of Pink's Three Dog Night Dog. Most people do not need to eat *three* hot dogs at one meal. But this is not just food; it's fun. It also costs more than a regular hot dog, so Pink's makes more money.

These "fun" foods often have a lot more fat and sugar in them. Look at the Three Dog Night Dog. Besides three hot dogs, you are eating a large tortilla, bacon, cheese, chili, and onions. You may not be hungry enough to eat three hot dogs covered in cheese and chili. But you order it (and eat it) anyway because it promises to be fun—an escape. It's like going to the movies or playing a video game, except this escape can make you obese.

Making food fun gives us the freedom to eat all the time. After all, you're supposed to eat when you're hungry. But you can have fun anytime! The food industry also encourages us to think of food as a reward we "deserve." It's a little bit of "me" time. You might know that you shouldn't eat that candy bar, but how can you deny yourself a little "me" time you "deserve"?

All the big food companies know this and use it to sell you food you *do not need*. It's not just fast food restaurants. Supermarket aisles are crowded with foods that promise you fun, like Keebler's Dippables. These snacks claim to "put fun back in food."

Monster Meals

Once you think of food as fun, you have no reason to stop eating. After all, if you're just a little hungry, it doesn't make sense to eat a lot of food. But if you're having a little fun, why not have a *lot* of fun?

Amherst, Massachusetts, is a college town, and the students there flock to Antonio's Pizza. Of course, Antonio's offers a lot more than regular plain pizza. Their pizzas include beef taco, potato and bacon, chicken quesadilla, and one that comes with a mix of ground beef, pepperoni, sausage, bacon, and extra cheese. Where is the pizza under all that food? It doesn't matter—you're having fun.

Another Amherst restaurant named Fatzo's (don't think about that name) offered a burger called "Mac the Knife." That's a hamburger topped with macaroni and cheese. It's like two meals in one! Except why do you need to eat two meals at once? Is that "fun" or is it a way to get obese very quickly?

Walk into any fast food restaurant and you will find the same thing: Monster meals loaded with sugar, fat, and salt.

• • • • • • • • • • • • • • • • •

▶ OVEREATING AS ENTERTAINMENT ◀

Is overeating fun? Some folks seem to think so. The Travel TV network has a show called *Man v. Food*. The host travels around the country and tries to swallow the biggest local meal he can find. And you can play along in the *Man v. Food* challenge. Here's what they want you to do: "Nosh down burgers, pizza, and other delicious treats until you pop. Build the tallest stack and then scramble to eat it all before time runs out."

Man v. Food is just one example of overeating as entertainment. Nathan's Hot Dogs has its annual hot dog eating contest. The winner in 2011 ate sixty-two hot dogs and buns in ten minutes! By the way, eating that much in a short time can actually be very dangerous. In order to compete, eating contestants have to train their stomachs to stretch, and they have to train themselves to ignore feelings of being full.

- Hardee's has a burger called the Monster Thickburger. It comes covered with bacon, cheese, and mayonnaise *and* butter. That's 1,420 calories in one sandwich. Remember, most adults only need about 2,000 calories a day! And we haven't counted the fries or the milk shake.
- The International House of Pancakes has cinnamon raisin French toast stuffed with sweet cream cheese; smothered with powdered sugar, fruit topping, and whipped topping; and served with two eggs, hash brown potatoes, and a choice of two strips of bacon or two sausage links.
- A breakfast sandwich from Burger King contains four eggs, four strips of bacon, and four slices of cheese.
- Starbucks offers a Strawberries & Creme Frappuccino with whipped cream and *eighteen* teaspoons of sugar. This "drink" contains more calories than a personal-size pepperoni pizza, and more sugar than six scoops of ice cream.

• • • • • • • • • • • • • • • •

More of Everything

Everywhere you turn, Americans are eating more of everything. By far the largest increase has been in fats and oils. Today, Americans eat 63 percent more fats and oils than they did 30 years ago. The use of sugars and sweeteners is also up 19 percent. We're also eating 43 percent more grain and 7 percent more meat, eggs, and nuts. We eat 24 percent more vegetables, which seems like good news until you learn a lot of those vegetables are french fries.

Americans have always eaten some foods that are loaded with sugar, fat, and salt. The grilled cheese sandwich and the milk shake have been around for decades. But today, these loaded and layered foods have become a large part of the American diet. And it's not just in fast food restaurants.

Supermarket foods have changed, too. Instead of buying potatoes in the produce section, we buy precooked potatoes in the frozen food aisle. A baked potato has no sugar or fat in it. Bags of frozen potatoes "au gratin" or french fries come with fat and sugar already added. Instead of plain frozen vegetables, we can buy our veggies glazed or smothered in cheese and butter sauces.

Leave the frozen food and you'll see the same thing in other aisles. Pasta sauce is often loaded with sugar. Or look at the breakfast cereals. It used to be a big deal to get two ingredients in one box, like Raisin Bran. Today, food companies load cereals with lots of extra flavors—and lots of sugar. Think of Lucky Charms, Cocoa Puffs, Honey Nut Cheerios, and of course, the lab rats' favorite—Froot Loops.

Take a look at the boxes. Do you notice the bright colors, the funny characters, the photographs of bowls of cereal? They are all there to make the cereal seem like *fun*. You are no longer eating because you're hungry, or even because the food tastes good—you're eating for fun, and there is no limit to the amount of fun (or food) you can have.

CHAPTER 13

Never Satisfied

Eating in America is less and less about satisfying hunger. Instead, we eat to satisfy cravings. We crave the mix of flavors, the feel of food going down easily. You may feel this as being hungry, but it's not the same thing. When you're really hungry, your body doesn't just want food, it *needs* food.

Highly processed food never leaves us satisfied. That is not an accident. This food is *designed* to not satisfy us—to leave us wanting more. It is designed to stimulate your desire—to make you want more.

☞ **Our food is easy to eat, but leaves us wanting more.**

Really Fast Food

Our food is processed, broken down, and pre-chewed. It's so easy to chew, it's almost like adult baby food. You don't have to think about it—just put it in your mouth, and it's gone before you know it. This easy-to-chew food is another reason people are eating too much.

Chewing and eating slowly helps you get the feeling of being "full." If you eat slowly, you will get that feeling in time to stop eating before you overeat. But if you eat quickly, you will keep eating past that point. You will eat more than your body needs. When you're eating a Monster Thickburger, you can easily wolf down almost a whole day's worth of calories in a couple of minutes.

Cole slaw is basically a salad of cabbage, carrots, and other vegetables. Old-fashioned coleslaw took a while to chew, and it really filled you up. Today, most coleslaw is chopped into very small pieces and mixed with lots of high-fat dressing. That salad has become a high-calorie food that goes down fast with less chewing. You can eat a lot more of it before you feel full, and you're swallowing more calories with every bite.

Compare apples to applesauce. An apple is full of flavor and no fat. But you have to bite into it and chew it. So food companies process the apple. First they get rid of the peel, which has a lot of the fiber and other nutrients. Then they mash the apple up until you don't have to chew it. Then they add sugar. Eat an apple and you will start to feel full. Eat a cup of applesauce and you won't be satisfied.

All this easy-to-eat food is no accident. Food industry experts have made it easier and easier to get a lot of calories from food with hardly any work at all. But foods that go "whoosh" don't leave us with a sense of being well fed. We eat so quickly, we no longer pay attention to what or how much we're eating. We're just shoveling the food in without thinking.

Give Them What They Want?

The food industry doesn't force anyone to buy their products. As far as they are concerned, they're just giving us what we want. Like the makers of Cinnabon, they are just making food that people like. If people like the food a little (or a lot) too much, it just proves that it's good—right?

But it's not as simple as that. The food companies don't just make food that people like. They make food that we cannot resist. For many people, once they get in the habit of eating these foods, it is almost impossible to stop. These foods are *bad for us*. That's a very important point. These foods are manufactured in a way that makes them harmful. The food companies are making billions of dollars by getting people to eat so much they become overweight and obese.

They've even figured out how to sell food to people who are worried about eating too much. I have a lot of experience with one of these foods—SnackWell's nonfat cookies. In spite of being no-fat, these cookies had gotten hold of me.

Time and again I'd eat one, walk away from the box, and return a few minutes later for another. And another. And another one after that. I didn't like my behavior, but I kept doing it anyway. Often I didn't even realize how many cookies I'd eaten until they were all gone. So when I got the chance to meet one of the people responsible for these cookies, I was very eager to talk to him.

Robert Smith was a vice president for research and development at Nabisco. He had helped create two of the company's bestsellers—Oreos and Chips Ahoy! Smith told me that Nabisco had a lot of trouble creating a no-fat cookie that people wanted to eat. Without fat, the cookie seemed tasteless and dry. Then scientists at the company found a fat substitute that did the trick. They combined it with the right flavors and textures, and they had a winner. They had created a no-fat cookie that had the same effect as a regular high-fat cookie. It makes people want to keep eating whether they are hungry or not.

The SnackWell's nonfat cookies are supposed to be a kind of diet food. After all, they're fat free, aren't they? But they've been designed to be like all of Nabisco's cookies—hard to resist. And so I found myself out of control whenever I saw them. I kept eating them.

In America, even our diet food makes us want to eat more.

CHAPTER 14

We Don't Know What We Want

Food companies spend a lot of time and money testing their products. They gather consumers together, give them samples, and ask for reactions. Isn't that proof they are just giving us what we want? Not really. The food companies aren't really testing what we want. They're testing to see if we can resist their new products or not. If people can resist the product, then the company has more work to do. If the food is irresistible, then they know they have a winner.

One problem is many of us don't *know* what we want. We crave these foods; we feel we *have* to have them. At the same time, we know these foods are bad for us. So we feel out of control. We want them, but we don't *want* to want them.

In food industry tests, this problem comes up all the time. For example, people in these tests say they are trying to avoid foods with a lot of fat. Yet they almost always prefer foods with more fat. People know they shouldn't have a lot of sugar, but they almost always prefer drinks with a lot of sugar. After they have high-sugar drinks, they sometimes can't tell if they're still thirsty or not. The drink *has not satisfied* their thirst. But they know they liked the drink.

We are so confused, sometimes we don't even recognize what we're eating. Many people know they shouldn't be eating snacks with a lot of salt. But they still crave the taste of salt. If you give them a high-salt snack but don't tell them what's in it, they will like it. And here's the strange part—they will say they like the snack because it *doesn't* have a lot of salt.

They're not lying when they say they think the chip is low-salt. They're just very confused. Their brains are split. One half likes the taste of salt; the other half knows that too much salt is bad for you.

☞ **We don't know what we are eating.**

They **Know What We Want**

Most of the time, we don't know why we crave certain foods. The food is working on a part of our brain, but we're not even aware of what is happening. We know we like it, but we really can't say why.

At taste tests, people have trouble explaining why they like a food. No one says, I liked that cookie because it had so much fat in it. Instead, people say, "I like it because it tastes good." If you ask them exactly what about the cookie tasted good, they won't be able to tell you. They'll just say something like "It was yummy." Only a food expert would be able to tell you the cookie was "yummy" because it had the right mix of sugar, fat, and salt.

The food industry relies on our confusion. They know most people will never recognize the high levels of sugar, fat, and salt in our food. Here's a test for you: Do you think bread has a lot of salt in it? In fact, most bread is highly salted. People prefer the taste of highly salted bread, *without knowing it*. But bread companies know it and so they add salt. Some bread also has a lot of sugar. A McDonald's hamburger bun is a good example. It has a fairly high level of sugar.

Did you know that ketchup has sugar in it and so does the sauce on a Pizza Hut pizza? You may know that crackers are salty, but did you know many of them contain a lot of fat and sugar? Ranch salad dressing has sugar in it, too. Put that on your salad, and you're just using lettuce to deliver sugar, fat, and salt.

Food companies try to hide the large amounts of sugar they put in products. The law says that ingredients on a label must be listed by the amount used. If sugar is the main ingredient in your breakfast cereal, sugar has to be listed first. So food companies have figured out a way around the law. Sugar goes by many different names. Instead of just using white refined sugar, food companies might also use brown sugar, high fructose corn syrup, honey, and molasses. Each one is listed separately on the label. The cereal contains the same amount of sweetness and calories, but now they are spread out in the list of ingredients. Most important, sugar is no longer the first thing on the list.

Even then you don't get the full picture. The Kellogg's Frosted Flakes label, for example, says that the cereal has 11 grams of sugar per serving. But nowhere does it tell you that the cereal is more than one-third added sugar.

The Battle for Your Brain

Food industry experts may not know the details of brain chemistry, but they know what works. They know which combinations of sugar, fat, and salt we crave. These combinations work on our brains, make us want to eat, even if another part of our brains know we shouldn't.

Michele Foley is a food scientist at Frito-Lay. Her job is to design foods that are, in her words, "simply irresistible." Through product testing and research, she has worked out the combinations of flavors, tastes, and textures that will make people crave Frito-Lay chips. Like other food industry scientists, she has discovered that these five things will make people crave food:

- Calories—the food must be high in sugar and fat
- Flavor "hits"—the food must deliver layers of strong flavors
- The first taste—the food must deliver a strong flavor right away
- Ease of eating—it must be easy to chew
- Melting away—the food must go down easily and quickly

All together, Foley says, "It's about creating a lot of fun in your mouth."

Once you know this, you can begin to understand why a food like Nacho Cheese Doritos is so powerful. It is high in calories, with a lot of fat and salt. It has layers of different flavors, from three different kinds of cheese, plus other dairy products.

Foley told me that by the time Fritos releases a new chip, they make "sure" that most people will find them irresistible. That is what the testing is really for. They don't test to figure out what we want. They test to figure out what we can't resist.

The payoff is huge. Food companies make food that most people just can't resist. Then they make billions of dollars selling us that food.

By the way, can you guess which Fritos chip people find easiest to resist? It's Baked Lay's Potato Chips. Those chips have a simple flavor, and don't have as much fat and don't melt away in the mouth. Lay's makes these chips because there's a market for people who want to eat healthier but still want their potato chips. But it turns out that healthier chips are less likely to make you overeat.

CHAPTER 15

It's All American Food Now

In some places in the world, people still eat traditional food. Those are foods whose recipes have been handed down from generation to generation. Whether they are the traditional foods of China or Mexico or the Middle East, they all have one thing in common. The foods and spices may be different but the meals are meant to satisfy your hunger and make you feel full.

But something strange happens to food from other countries when it travels to the United States. The meals become Americanized. Extra sugar, fat, and salt get added to the recipes. The food may look like something they'd eat in China or Mexico, but it no longer tastes like the original.

From Taco Bell to the nearest Japanese restaurant, the world's food is turning into American food. And it works the other way, too. We are exporting our high-sugar, high-fat food to other countries. American fast food chains are busy spreading across the globe. For example, China now has more than 3,800 Kentucky Fried Chicken and Pizza Hut locations.

☞ **American style food, high in sugar, fat and salt, is spreading across the globe.**

Fat Sushi

Sushi is a classic Japanese dish. It is basically raw fish served on rice. Sometimes it is wrapped in seaweed. Traditional sushi is about as fat-free a meal as you can have. But in the United States, sushi has mutated. Now you can get sushi made with cream cheese (called Philly rolls). There's also sushi with battered and fried shrimp topped with mayonnaise. American teriyaki sauce has far more sugar than anything you'll find in Japan.

Chinese food has also become more "American." Traditional Chinese dishes have more vegetables and less sugar than "Chinese" food in the United States. That's why some Chinese restaurants in the United States have two different menus. One is for Chinese customers and one for Americans. The Chinese customers want real Chinese food, not American style. As the owner of a Chinese restaurant in Connecticut told me, "When I look at American Chinese food, I think it is not Chinese."

The dish we call "General Tso's Chicken" was invented in China in an area called Hunan. But cooks in America load the dish with sugar. The chef who invented General Tso's Chicken says it's not the same in the United States. "The dish can't be sweet," he says. "The taste of Hunan cuisine is not sweet."

And, of course, Chinese-style fast food is even worse. Panda Express is the nation's largest Chinese restaurant chain. In 2007, it sold more than $1 billion worth of food. But is it really Chinese food or is it just more high-sugar, high-fat, and high-salt American food?

The Orange Chicken they sell is made in the Panda Express factory. The dark chicken chunks are injected with water, oil, and salt. Then they are battered and fried in oil. At the restaurants, the meat is deep-fried in oil again for at least five minutes. Then it's coated with a high sugar sauce. In the end, your "Chinese food" is full of the same old trio—sugar, fat, and salt.

The same thing goes for the Panda Express spring rolls. Sugar is listed twice on the ingredient list. Salt is listed two times while fat makes an appearance in four places. Those frozen spring rolls arrive at Panda Express restaurants with instructions to deep-fry them in oil for five to six minutes.

Feed the World?

Meanwhile, American food companies are busy expanding in other countries. They are trying to sell foods loaded with sugar, fat, and salt to everyone on the globe. A few years ago, I visited health clinics in South Africa. Many of them were in very poor areas. A lot of the people visiting the clinics were suffering from HIV infection. Yet I also saw some very obese people. Even some of the nurses and other health care workers were obese. I asked a doctor to explain what I was seeing. The answer was simple, she said. Kentucky Fried Chicken had come to town.

According to the World Health Organization:

- Worldwide obesity has more than doubled since 1980.
- In 2008, 1.5 billion adults were overweight. Of those, over 200 million men and nearly 300 million women were obese.
- Nearly 43 million children under the age of five were overweight in 2010.
- In many countries, being overweight and obese kills more people than hunger.

Over one billion adults are obese. At the same time, about one billion people around the world struggle with hunger. About 4 million children die every year because they don't get enough to eat. So we have to ask ourselves, does the world really need more food loaded with sugar, fat, and salt? Do poor nations really need to add the health problems of obesity to all of the other problems they face? Do we really want a world where people are dying because they have too little food while other people are dying because they have too much?

Just don't ask American food companies that question. They are too busy exporting our high-sugar, high-fat food to the rest of the world.

CHAPTER 16

Fake Food

We no longer eat just because we're hungry. Our food is no longer meant to satisfy us. Instead it is designed to turn us into endless eaters. It makes me wonder: If food doesn't satisfy your hunger, then is it food anymore?

I know one thing for certain. A lot of the ingredients food companies use *aren't* real food. Artificial chemicals, flavors, and additives are in almost all of our processed food. These chemicals don't exist in nature. They are not part of a traditional healthy diet. But food companies add them to our food because they are good for business. They are cheaper than real foods. Plus they add flavors that work on our brains and make foods hard to resist.

☞ Food companies use chemical flavors
to make food hard to resist.

Chocolate Without Chocolate

I went to an annual meeting of the Institute of Food Technologists in New Orleans. What's a food technologist? It's someone who designs processed foods for food companies. I walked along the long line of booths and displays. At one booth, someone handed me a frozen chocolate drink to taste. From the first sip I knew it was something special. The chocolate taste seemed to explode on my tongue.

But was there chocolate in the drink? The ingredient list said it contained chocolate fudge caramel flavor, granulated sugar, cocoa powder, nonfat dry milk, dextrose, heavy cream, salt, and artificial flavor.

Cocoa powder is one form of chocolate. It was the third ingredient on the list, after sugar. But that didn't tell me how much was in the drink. So I asked the food scientist at the booth, "How much cocoa powder is in here?"

"Very little," she answered.

Where did the chocolate taste come from? From the "chocolate fudge caramel flavor." What is that exactly? It's something cooked up in a laboratory to taste like chocolate.

"Our business is to make something taste like something, even if it is not," the food scientist explained.

Smoke Without Fire

So it turns out that even huge amounts of sugar, fat, and salt aren't enough. To make a food even more impossible to resist, you need to add chemical flavoring. Artificial flavors are everywhere. Take the Oreo cookie, for example. It gets its flavor from sugar and corn syrup (sugar), oil (fat), salt, and artificial vanilla flavoring.

Food companies use these chemicals because they are cheaper than natural flavors. Chemicals also allow companies to create flavor combinations that don't exist in nature. Do you like the sound of blueberry lavender, chocolate espresso chipotle, or pear apricot ginger? They all can be whipped up in the laboratory. Food scientists like to add unusual flavors to food. The strange tastes excite our brains and make food hard to resist.

One food scientist told me that people like smoky flavors. But you don't need real smoke to get that taste. You can add "smoke" flavor from a bottle. You can choose from hickory smoke flavor, roast turkey flavor, fire-roasted garlic, roast chicken flavor, or dozens of others. You can make food taste like it's been grilled even if it was never near a fire.

To save money, food manufacturers can replace real fruit with a manufactured fruit taste. Instead of butter, manufacturers can use something called Butter Plus. One pound of Butter Plus replaces fifty pounds of real butter.

Then there are the cheese flavorings sold by Kraft. You can buy blue cheese flavor, American cheese flavor, and cream cheese flavors. But none of them contain much cheese. Kraft says its dairy flavors are designed "to deliver cheese flavor in any product application," making it possible to reduce "the cheese and dairy content of your products without sacrificing flavor." That means your food can taste like cheese but you don't have to pay for real cheese.

There is a giant industry devoted to developing fake flavorings for food. These flavors supply variety that doesn't exist in real food. They have super-charged tastes and textures in a way that real food does not. As one flavor company representative told me: "We transform technology into good taste. Tastes to excite, stimulate, comfort, and linger."

Is It Food?

These artificial flavorings are added to high-sugar, high-fat foods to make them even more irresistible. Not only are these fake foods loaded in calories, they also have less of the important nutrients your body needs. Real fruit has loads of vitamins and minerals. Fake fruit just has calories. Of course, real cheese does have fat in it, but it also has a lot of protein, calcium, and other important minerals. The fake cheese has none of those things.

Most people don't really know what is in our food. We don't read the labels, or if we do, we don't understand what we're reading. We are eating huge amounts of this stuff, but we don't know what it is.

Sometimes I don't know what it is, either. Is it food? Or is it just a way of delivering chemicals to your brain?

CHAPTER 17

Perfect Food

Have you ever baked cookies at home? No matter how hard you try, each cookie comes out a little different than the next. Some are bigger. Some are crispier. Some come out moister. Some might even get burned a little. We know that home cooked food is like that. Each batch is a little different.

Supermarket food and meals at fast food restaurants are the opposite. When you open a bag of cookies from the store, all the cookies are exactly the same. The food companies make sure their products are uniform. Each one tastes the same and looks the same as the last one you had.

They can do this because our processed food is manufactured in large factories. The burgers, fried chicken, donuts, and even the salads you buy at fast food restaurants are mass produced on assembly lines. Much of it is shipped frozen to the restaurant where it is thawed out. Sometimes it's fried or cooked again.

Mass-produced food is cheaper to make. It also gives the

manufacturer a lot of control over the taste and appearance of the product. But this food is not healthy for you. In fact, it is not meant to be healthy for you. It is designed with one thing in mind: to get you to come back again and again.

☞ **Processed food is manufactured in factories with large amounts of sugar, fat, salt, and chemicals.**

New and Boring

A lot of food is advertised as "exciting" or "new." In reality, processed food is very boring. Every Big Mac looks and tastes the same. Every Dunkin' Donuts chocolate donut looks and tastes the same. An egg roll at a Chili's in Des Moines tastes the same as one in San Diego. And they are meant to be that way.

Food manufacturers make sure their products are standard and predictable. They use modern technology to smooth out the flavors. They adjust their machines to get the exact, right amount of sugar, fat, salt, and chemical additives. They make sure each cookie or burger or egg roll looks the way it does in the advertisements.

They also make sure that the taste is the same throughout. In a cookie you baked at home, one part might be a little more cooked than another. One bite might have more chips in it than another. But manufactured cookies are the same all the way through. Their chips and their flavor are evenly spread out.

Food companies don't want you to have any surprises when you eat their products. Once you've been conditioned by the taste of a cookie or a hamburger, they make sure you have that same experience every time. They do this so you keep *coming back for more.*

Fried, Frozen, Fried

What happens in many restaurants isn't exactly cooking. It's more like the food is precooked at the factory and then put together at the restaurant. Even a plate of nachos is often made this way. It is put together with pre-fried tortilla chips, frozen or canned jalapeno peppers, and packaged cheese mixes. Likewise, steaks and other meats are usually trimmed, seasoned, and sealed in a vacuum package to preserve color and flavoring. At the restaurant all they have to do is open the package and put it on the grill.

Those chicken nuggets look deliciously golden brown and tender. However, they began their life in a factory far away. You might think that nugget is a piece of chicken, but it is not. It is *made* from chopped chicken and pressed together with lots of other ingredients, including water, oil, and chemicals.

Each nugget is coated with batter, then fried, then "quick frozen." That means it is blasted with cold air, cold nitrogen, or cold carbon dioxide as it travels along a conveyor belt. They are shipped in bags to the restaurant, where they are fried again. A lot of the frozen foods in your supermarket, like frozen french fries, are made this way, too. You might be eating a lot of factory-made food at home.

By the way, a lot of school cafeterias make their meals this way. The food they serve is often factory made, precooked, frozen, and then thawed out at school.

Cheap and Unhealthy

Factory-made food *is* cheaper than handmade food. When machines are doing the chopping, frying, and other chores, it saves money. Thanks to factory-made food, Americans can afford to eat high-sugar, high-fat meals like never before. In fact, high-sugar, high-fat foods are often cheaper than whole fruits, grains, and vegetables.

Price is one thing that big food companies brag about. They say they are providing cheap food to people. That is true. The question we have to ask is, what is the point of food if it doesn't make you healthy and just makes you want to eat more?

As we've seen, their factory-made food is *not* healthy. It's loaded with sugar, fat, and salt. Many of the vitamins, minerals, and other healthy nutrients have been stripped away. It's not fresh because it's been frozen and shipped over long distances. Plus, it's been designed to make you overeat, leading to obesity. It might be a little cheaper than good, healthy food, but when you think about how it is making you sick, it's not much of a bargain, is it?

That's why some schools are going back to the old way of

making meals for their students. They've stopped buying frozen bags of precooked meals. Instead, they are buying fresh vegetables, meat, and grain and cooking them right in the school cafeteria. These dishes won't be loaded with sugar, fat, salt, and chemicals. They won't work on your brain to make you keep eating. Instead, they will do what food is supposed to do—make you healthy and satisfied.

CHAPTER 18

Getting You Hooked

We've seen that processed food is all about one thing—getting you to eat. The way the food is designed, cooked, sold, and advertised is all meant to make you keep eating. As far as the food companies are concerned, the more you eat, the better. One food executive I talked to put it very bluntly.

"The goal is to get you hooked," he told me.

Food industry people also use words like "irresistibility" and "craveability." They are very clear that their main goal is to make you crave their foods so you will keep eating.

☞ The food industry's goal is to keep you eating.

Supersize!

One well-known marketing trick is to "supersize" your meal. Giant dishes heaped with food are exciting. Plus giant portions make you feel you're getting a good deal. The extra food doesn't really cost the restaurant that much. They can offer to super-size your meal for just a few cents more and still make a nice profit. Of course, giant portions also make you eat more than you need.

To supersize cheaply, companies replace real ingredients with fake ones. Thirty years ago, a chocolate muffin was made with real eggs, real chocolate, and real butter. It was rich and flavorful, but it was also small—two ounces. Then companies realized that they could make a five-ounce muffin for pennies more. But to do that, they couldn't use real butter. Instead of eggs, they use powdered egg substitutes. The flavor came from chemicals. But it sure was big.

I talked to a man who used to work for Coca-Cola. He told me how the soft drink companies work to get us to drink more soda. A regular serving used to be eight ounces. You can hardly find an eight-ounce soft drink anymore. The large size used to be sixteen ounces. Now the large size is thirty-two ounces—a full quart of sugar and water. The extra sugar costs a few pennies. But the companies can charge you an extra 50 cents or more for the supersize drink. That's almost all profit.

The Taco Chip Challenge

By now I think you have gotten the idea. The food industry is out to get you. They spend literally *billions* of dollars on research. They design, test, and market food that you can't resist. The result is that you are fighting a many-headed monster. It's a monster that is trying to get you to eat nonstop. And too many of us are losing the battle.

Think of it as the taco chip challenge. Can you pass a plate of taco chips without eating one? Can you eat one without eating a dozen? Do you eat a dozen without even realizing what you are doing? Many of us just can't resist. And now, those plates of taco chips are *everywhere*.

Maybe it's not taco chips. Maybe it's the Cinnabon bakery in every mall. Or the Dunkin' Donuts on every corner. Or the candy bars in every type of store, newsstand, or vending machine. Every single day and every single place you go, processed food is there. The food is cheap, it's easy to eat, and most of all, you crave it.

With a giant industry working day and night to get us to eat more, no wonder so many of us are overweight and obese. Many of us just can't resist food. We eat all the time. We have become *overeaters*.

PART THREE

UNDERSTANDING OVEREATING

CHAPTER 19

The Signs of Overeating

We've seen how sugar, fat, and salt work on the brain to make us crave food. We've also seen how food companies use this to get us to buy their products. Both of these lead to the core subject of this book—overeating.

Overeating is very common in America today. I think it is the most important reason so many of us are overweight and obese. And I know that overeating is something that people can learn to control and stop. But before we can end overeating, we have to understand exactly what it is. How do we recognize it?

Overeating is not the same as eating too much. Everyone eats too much from time to time. When you feel very full after a big meal, you might say, "I ate too much." But what I call *overeating* is something else. Overeating is when you feel out of control with food. It's when you eat all the time, sometimes without even knowing it. It's when you feel full and you keep on eating. It's when you eat even when you're not hungry.

☞ **Overeating is when people feel driven to eat even when they're not hungry.**

Why Do People Gain Weight?

I know I said this earlier. But I am going to repeat myself because I think it's very important. There have been a lot of different explanations of why people gain weight. But the research is quite clear. People gain weight because they *eat too much*.

Obese people eat more than people who are not obese. This is a fact. Sometimes this doesn't show up in studies because often people are not honest about how much they eat. Either they're embarrassed or they really don't know how much they're eating. But if they carefully track what they're eating, it becomes very obvious.

Overweight and obese people eat too much at meals. They also eat when it's not mealtime. They eat snacks throughout the day. They may eat extra meals in the evening or at night. Hungry or not, full or not, they just keep eating.

Obese people are also willing to work hard to get the foods they crave. In one study, two groups of women earned points that could be traded for prizes. One group was obese; the other was not. Sometimes the prize was a high-sugar, high-fat snack food. At other times, the prize was an activity like playing video games, or watching TV sitcoms. The obese women worked much harder to get points when the prize was a food loaded and layered with sugar, fat, and salt. They craved the food even though they weren't hungry.

Now I want to repeat something else I said earlier, which is also very important—eating is good for you! You are *supposed* to eat when you're hungry. Eating good food should be enjoyable. I hope you enjoy your food and find pleasure in a good meal. The problem comes when people lose control and have to eat all the time, even when they're not hungry. That is overeating.

• • • • • • • • • • • • • • • •

▶ **CHARACTERISTICS OF OVEREATERS** ◀

- Feeling out of control with food
- Difficulty controlling your eating
- Hard time "stopping" eating
- Thinking about food a lot

• • • • • • • • • • • • • • • •

Who Is Overeating?

About 50 percent of all obese people have these characteristics. About 30 percent of overweight people also have at least two of these habits. That shows a very strong connection between these behaviors and being overweight or obese. Overeaters are likely to say things like: "When it comes to foods I love, I have no willpower," and "I have days when I can't seem to think about anything else but food."

About 17 percent of *thin* people also have these characteristics. Why aren't they overweight? They have other behaviors that keep their weight in check. These people are at risk of becoming overweight.

This is especially important for young people. You might not be overweight now, but you might already be overeating. If you continue to overeat, you could become overweight or obese as an adult.

Overeating in Kids

Younger and younger children are becoming overeaters. This is very alarming. Kids who overeat are in great danger of becoming overweight or obese. They are at great risk for developing diabetes and other diseases. And they are likely to struggle with overeating for the rest of their lives.

Overeating in kids is something very new. In fact, it is shocking to many scientists that kids can overeat at all. Scientists always thought that we were born with a natural ability to regulate the amount of food we eat.

Infants and preschool children will naturally adjust how much they eat to get just the amount of calories they need. If you feed a two-year-old something with a lot of calories, they will eat less during the rest of the day. They don't eat more because *they are not hungry.* Their bodies recognize the feeling of being full, and they don't want more food.

But something is happening to kids to upset that natural balance. Over the past twenty years, very young children in America have begun to overeat.

I spoke about this with Susan Johnson, a scientist at the University of Colorado. She told me that in the 1980s, children aged two to four were not overeating. If you fed them extra calories, they would balance that out by eating less. By the 1990s, this was no longer true. Many children could no longer adjust their eating to stay in balance. If they ate extra calories, later in the day they might eat a little less, but not enough to balance out the extra food.

Johnson now sees three- and four-year-olds who are able to eat very large meals. These little kids sometimes eat as much as 800 calories in one sitting. They just keep asking for more. "I did not see this kind of behavior in the past," she told me.

Johnson also studied children aged five to twelve. She tested them with two different fruit-flavored drinks. The drinks tasted the same, but one had a lot more calories than the other. She wanted to see if kids who had the high-calorie drink would eat less during the day. She found that younger kids who had the high-calorie drink would eat a little less during the day. But they still wound up eating more than they needed.

For example, after drinking a high-calorie beverage, five-year-old girls ate less of other foods, but they still wound up eating more, by about 20 percent. Eight-year-old girls who had the high-calorie drink adjusted less. They were eating 40 percent more than they needed. Eleven-year-olds did even worse. The ones who had the high-calorie drink wound up eating 70 percent more than they needed. In other words, as kids got older, they were losing the ability to stop eating when they felt full.

Johnson found this very surprising. She told me, "I never saw children who ate and ate and ate until you finally had to cut them off and say, 'You're done.' They are eating to excess now."

Other studies have shown the same thing. Some kids are losing the ability to know when they are full. They will eat as much food as is put in front of them. They will eat all day long. They eat when they are not hungry. They have become overeaters.

CHAPTER 20

Trained to Eat

When I first began to talk to people about overeating, they had two reactions. Many people immediately understood what I was talking about. They had felt the loss of control themselves. They often found it impossible to resist foods even though they knew they were eating too much.

The second, smaller group had a different reaction. They didn't understand what I was talking about. They had no trouble resisting food. They were convinced that people overate because they were weak. They didn't have enough willpower.

Even many of the overeaters felt that way. They felt it was their fault that they couldn't stop eating. They felt bad about themselves. They wanted to be stronger, but somehow they couldn't.

To me, this is one of the most important discoveries I made about overeating. People don't overeat because they are weak. It's not from lack of willpower. People overeat because their brains are wired to crave foods loaded with sugar, fat, and salt.

They have become conditioned to eat whether they are hungry or not.

☞ **Overeating is the result of changes
in the reward center of the brain.**

Change in the Brain

Why do some people eat even though they are not hungry? As we learned in Part One, loaded and layered food (food that contains lots of sugar, fat, and salt) trigger the brain's reward center. Then the reward center in our brains naturally drives us to seek out that reward again. That is the craving that some people feel for loaded and layered processed food. It is the brain's reward center telling them to work hard to get that reward again.

That is why I say that overeating is *reward-driven* eating. When you overeat, you eat for the feeling of eating, not because you need food.

What loaded and layered foods do to the brain is similar to the effect of addictive drugs. After a while, the brain becomes *conditioned* to want and expect this reward. You could say the brain has been *trained* to react to these foods.

When the brain is conditioned in this way, real chemical and physical changes take place. When we look at brain scans of people who overeat, we can see the changes quite clearly. First, the reward centers in their brains light up when they get a food cue. We can see on the brain scan that the cue makes the neurons in the reward center very active. These neurons become more active than in people who are not overeaters.

There is a biological reason why overeaters overeat. When exposed to food cues, their brains' reward centers are hyper-reactive, and when they start eating, their brains' reward centers stay activated until all the food is gone.

People with these brain patterns will eat whenever they have the chance. It doesn't matter if they've just eaten. They respond to the cues of food by eating.

Nature or Nurture?

Why do some people become overeaters and others do not? Is overeating genetic? Is it something you are born with? Or is overeating something you learn by being around other people who overeat? Do you learn it from the intense marketing carried on by the food industry? We don't yet have the answers to these questions.

My guess is that some people are born with genes that make them more likely to become conditioned by rewards such as high-sugar, high-fat foods. But genes are not enough to make them overeaters. In order to become an overeater, you need to have lots of food available, including foods that are high in sugar, fat, and salt. It is only when you are constantly surrounded with these foods that overeating becomes possible.

Nonstop Eating

And we *are* constantly surrounded by loaded and layered foods. Food is everywhere, and it is relatively inexpensive. The number of neighborhood food stores and restaurants has exploded. Everywhere you go, you see vending machines, convenience stores, supermarkets, and fast food restaurants of every kind. Gas stations, drug stores, electronics stores, and just about every other kind of store also sell food.

And almost all of that food is loaded with sugar, fat, and salt.

Not so long ago it would have been considered weird to walk down the street drinking or eating a slice of pizza. Today, most of us wouldn't even notice someone doing that. We eat everywhere—in our cars, on the bus, walking down the street. Every time people get together, for any reason, there is food ready to be eaten.

A friend of mine from the Netherlands told me how strange this seems to her. "We go to a meeting in America and somebody will inevitably bring in a huge plate of bagels and cream cheese and muffins," she told me. "For Europeans it seems very odd, but it just seems to be expected here. Everybody seems to be expecting that a lot of food will suddenly show up."

When I was a kid, families ate meals together. Snacks were just for kids because it was felt they needed extra food to help them grow. Adults didn't eat snacks. Today, everyone snacks and we don't eat less at meals either.

If we even *have* meals. Today, many families seldom eat to-gether, and if they do, it's likely to be a take-out meal of pizza or fried chicken or burgers. Fewer people cook at home, unless you count microwaving something. That means our diet is more and more processed food, either from fast food restaurants or the frozen food section of the supermarket. All that processed food means we are eating too much sugar, fat, and salt at every meal.

CHAPTER 21

The Overeating Cycle

By now, you may have begun to understand why it is so hard to stop overeating. Willpower is not enough. Part of your brain knows that these foods are bad for you. At the same time, another part of your brain is sending out powerful signals driving you to get more of these foods. Part of your brain has become conditioned to be activated by these foods. Most of the time, the drive for reward, the *craving*, will win out.

I believe that overeaters like myself can retrain their brains. They can learn to weaken the drive from the reward center. They can change their conditioning. That will help put the conscious part of their brains back in control.

But before that can be done, it helps to understand exactly how the reward center in the brain works.

There are three parts to this:

- First, there are cues in our surroundings that trigger the reward center.

- Second, there is the strong effect of the first taste of a food.
- Third, there are negative emotions, like anger and worry, that drive us to eat.

If we understand how these three things work on our brains, we can begin to interrupt the brain's reward cycle. Then we can slow down or stop the reward center from driving us to eat.

☞ If we understand how the brain's reward center works, we can begin to stop overeating.

Start Eating!

You may know that on live television shows, the audience is often told when to laugh or applaud. Someone may even stand up in front of the audience with a sign that says, "Start applauding." That sign is a cue. When the audience sees the sign, it knows to begin applauding.

Foods can cue your brain in the same way. When you see a food cue, it's as if someone is holding up a sign telling your brain, "Start eating!"

On my way home from the gym, I drive past In-N-Out Burger. That's a very popular hamburger chain in the western United States. As I near the restaurant, I'm expecting to see it. I begin thinking about how good a hamburger and fries would taste. It's like someone has held up a sign that says, "Start eating!"

A debate begins inside my head.

Remember how good that was? Let's eat more.

No, we shouldn't.

It's soooo good. We need to get more.

But it's bad for us.

What are you talking about? It tastes really, really good. How can that be bad?

In the past, I often would have stopped for a hamburger and fries—even though *I was not hungry a minute before.*

For me, just knowing that the In-N-Out is about to appear is a strong enough cue to get that debate started. I have been conditioned by my past experiences with the food there to want to eat whenever I see it. Your cues may be different. There are thousands of other cues all around us. Often we are not even aware of them. Seemingly out of the blue, we may begin to think about a favorite sandwich or doughnut. We don't even know what got us thinking about it. But somewhere in our surroundings there was a cue.

If I make that stop at the In-N-Out often enough, it will become an automatic behavior, a habit. I know this sounds strange, but even my debate with myself can become another cue. It's like

I am writing a script that I will follow from now on. First I get close to the In-N-Out. Then I start craving the food. Then I have a debate with myself. Then I will lose the debate and eat.

Giving in to the reward center is a big relief. I no longer have to struggle against part of my brain. Knowing that I will feel relieved when I give in makes the food even harder to resist. That feeling of relief becomes part of the reward.

Bet You Can't Eat Just One

If you're an overeater, giving in to the cue is just the beginning. Another trigger is the very first taste of the food. You might have given in to your reward center by saying, "I'll just have one bite" or "I'll only eat one."

But of course, as the advertisement tells us, you can't eat just one. The first bite or taste of a food can be a powerful trigger that will drive you to eat more. You might think that a taste or a bite will satisfy you, but it has the opposite effect. That first taste *increases* your craving. It makes you want the food even more than you did before the first bite.

In animals or humans that lived thousands of years ago, that makes sense. It's a good survival reaction. If you taste a food and it is loaded with calories, your reward center drives you to get more of it. You wouldn't be able to overeat because the foods loaded with sugar and fat were rare. Today, that same reaction is a disaster. High-calorie food is all over, ready to be eaten; you can have as much as you want.

This reaction gets even stronger if you try to resist earlier cues. Say I manage to win the debate with my brain's reward center and I pass the In-N-Out. Then later in the day, I pass another In-N-Out, and this time I give in. Now that first taste of the hamburger is an even stronger trigger for overeating.

But this kind of trigger only works if there is more food available right away. If you eat one potato chip, you might wind up eating the whole bag—but only if there are more chips in the bag. If the bag is already empty, automatic eating will stop.

Eating for Stress

Emotions are a third trigger for overeating. People often experience this as "eating for stress." When some people feel angry, sad, or worried, they sometimes use food to change their mood. They eat to feel happier or to calm themselves down.

Remember, loaded and layered foods work on the reward center of our brains. They give us pleasure and make us feel better. If we are sad or angry, eating a cookie or other snack can change our mood. Over time, eating to relieve stress becomes another habit. Whenever you feel stressed, you will reach for a cookie, often without realizing what you are doing.

Of course, eating a cookie doesn't get rid of whatever was making you stressed in the first place. It just makes you feel better for a little while. If the stress is still there, then you will feel the urge to eat again, and very soon. And our anger with ourselves after eating what we shouldn't can add to our stress.

If we look at brain scans, we see very clear evidence that some people eat to change their moods. Scientists looked at people's brains when they were told they were about to get a milk shake. First the researchers asked some of the subjects to remember something very sad or tragic. Those people, who were feeling sad, had greater brain activity when they were told they would get a milk shake.

This is not true for everyone. Some people do not use food to change their moods. Those people are less likely to be over-eaters. But for many of us, bad moods and stress can be powerful triggers that make us seek high-sugar, high-fat food.

All of these responses quickly become automatic. We respond to these triggers by eating, often without realizing what we are doing. But once we *do* know what is happening, we can begin to change our behavior.

CHAPTER 22

How We Get Trapped

Now we begin to understand the cycle of overeating behavior. It goes like this:

Food Cues: Places, advertisements, smells, memories, and emotions trigger the brain's reward center.

Cravings: The reward center in the brain drives you to eat. You might try to resist, but eventually you give in.

Reward: You eat. The next time you are exposed to a food cue, it triggers the cycle again. Every time this happens, it strengthens the brain's response.

After a few cycles, this becomes a deeply fixed habit. Real biological changes take place in your brain. You become conditioned or trained. The habit becomes automatic. You become trapped in the cycle of overeating.

☞ Overeaters get trapped in a cycle
of automatic behavior.

Nothing Is More Important

There's another reason loaded and layered foods take over our brains. They trick our brains into thinking they're the most important thing around. Your brain focuses on the sugar, fat, and salt and pushes aside everything else. (A scientist would say you are focusing on the *salient stimulus*. That simply means focusing on the most important thing around.)

Focusing on the most important thing in our environment is wired into our brains. It's necessary for survival. Think about it. If your house is on fire, you need to focus on escaping. If you come face to face with a grizzly bear, you need to focus on that. If you are starving and you see some food, you need to focus on getting and eating that food.

In some people, loaded and layered food hijacks these brain circuits. Thoughts of the food push aside other thoughts. If we really were starving, or if we lived in the wilderness where high-calorie foods weren't available, this would make sense. If that was the case, we couldn't overeat. But we live in an environment where high-sugar, high-fat food is always available. It is not just about fat, sugar, and salt. It's the fact that fat, sugar, and salt is in all our food and the fact that food is everywhere.

I saw this in action recently. I was talking with someone at work, and I opened a box of chocolate-chip cookies. He sighed and asked, "Why did you have to do that?" The sight of the cookies was one of his food cues. Suddenly, the cookies became the most important, or *salient*, thing in the room for him. He had become conditioned to respond to the sight or smell of cookies by craving them. The response was automatic.

The Power of Memories

Memories play an important role in the cycle of overeating. A place, an advertisement, or something else triggers the memory of a loaded and layered food. The trigger might be something you do every day, like get out of school, walk past a store, turn on the television, or go into the kitchen.

The memory is powerful because it is a memory of a powerful reward—a food loaded with sugar, fat, and salt. We remember how that food tasted. Or we remember how it helped us feel better. Naturally, we want to feel better. It's only a short step from wanting it to feeling that we *need* it. This just increases our desire for the food. You begin a new cycle of craving, eating, and reward. Each time you go through the cycle, the memory gets stronger.

After you repeat this a few times, the cycle becomes wired into your brain. This is just the way your brain works. When

124

you repeat an action over and over, your brain remembers and begins to do it automatically. This saves you energy and effort. It's just like practicing a musical instrument or a sport, except you're practicing overeating. This is how we become conditioned overeaters.

Eating Without Thinking

Once we develop the habit of overeating, we repeat it without thinking. We eat just because that is what our brains have been conditioned to do. We eat literally without thinking. I know this has happened to me. I will find myself eating a cookie or a bag of snacks without ever making a conscious decision to eat.

In experiments with animals, once they developed the habit of overeating, they kept on eating even after the food made them sick. Their conditioning was so strong, they ignored what was happening to them.

It gets worse. Overeating leads to *more* overeating. When we are shoveling in the food, our brains go on "automatic pilot." When that happens we are like "zombies." When we come out of it, we ask "why did I just do that?"

We get stuck in a never-ending quest for bigger, sweeter, tastier rewards. And the rewards are all around us in the form of sugar, fat, and salt. But no matter how many rewards we get, the desire we have cannot be satisfied. The only things we get are a feeling of being out of control and the problems of being overweight or obese.

CHAPTER 23

Finding a Way Out

It is perfectly natural to like to eat. It is also perfectly natural to like foods that are high in sugar, fat, and salt. But there is a difference between liking a food and having a problem with food. As we've seen, people who overeat don't just like these foods—they cannot stop thinking about them. The desire pushes out other thoughts. They spend a lot of time and energy struggling against the craving and often losing.

For many overeaters, the mental battle is one of the worst things they experience. If you can't stop thinking about food, no matter how hard you try, after a short time you become depressed. You can't help wondering what is wrong with you. You begin to feel that you are a very weak person.

All of these unhappy thoughts lead the overeater to seek out something that will make him or her feel better. And what could be a better reward than a food loaded with sugar, fat, and salt—like a candy bar? The candy bar was the problem, but now it becomes the solution. The overeater feels that only a candy bar can bring relief. The overeater thinks, "I feel so awful now, but if I actually had that candy bar, I'd feel better."

This is one of the big problems with overeating. The more we struggle against it, the more we wind up trapped in the overeating cycle. Until we interrupt that cycle, we will continue to be trapped.

☞ **The way to end overeating is by interrupting the reward cycle in your brain.**

Don't Think of a White Bear!

The more you struggle against your cravings, the stronger they become. It's known as the white bear problem. If you tell yourself not to think about a white bear, soon that's all you can think about. It's very hard to make thoughts go away by fighting them. It's the same thing with eating. The more we try to push away thoughts of food, the stronger those thoughts become.

If we think the food is a delicious reward, then the problem gets worse. Part of you feels this is something really good. Another part of you thinks you shouldn't have it. This only makes you feel robbed or deprived. This is a very negative emotion, and we know that negative emotions lead some people to eat. After struggling and giving in, overeaters feel even worse about themselves, which of course leads to more eating.

People with these brain patterns might be able to stop overeating for a while. Many overeaters mange to go on a diet, even lose a lot of weight. It takes every ounce of willpower they have to stop overeating. But willpower is not enough. If their brain patterns aren't changed, then the old habits return and the weight comes right back.

Breaking the Cycle

How can we end this cycle of overeating? If struggling against all the thoughts and desires doesn't work, what does? Diets will work for a short time. But if you have not laid down new neural circuits, if there has not been new learning, after the diet your brain will just start responding to all the food cues again. The answer is to break the patterns that lead to overeating. This is not easy, but it can be done. Overeaters have to change their conditioning and what they want, and retrain their brains. We have to create new habits that lead to healthy eating.

PART FOUR

FOOD REHAB

CHAPTER 24

Learning How to Eat

I hope you haven't gotten the idea that overeating is so powerful that nothing can be done about it. I don't believe that at all. The whole point of learning about overeating and how it works is so we can use that knowledge to stop it. That's what the last part of this book is about.

It's true that overeating is based on our biology. Our brains are wired to like foods that are high in sugar, fat, and salt. But our brains contain a whole lot more than a simple program driving us to get sugar, fat, and salt. We can use our brains and our knowledge to stop overeating.

You may feel out of control with eating, but you are not a robot. You can change what, how, and when you eat, instead of having food control you.

☞ We can retrain our brains so that we are
in control of what, how, and when we eat.

Making New Habits

Habits like overeating can be very strong. They can't be changed quickly. Even if you're still young, you may have been practicing overeating for years. Each time you go through the cycle of overeating, it just makes the habit stronger. So breaking the habit may take some time.

But remember, you *learned* how to overeat. You learned by repeating your overeating patterns until they became automatic. And those patterns are not simply learned, they are also driven. You may not have been aware of what you were doing, but that's what you did. So if you learned to overeat, there's no reason you can't learn *not* to overeat. To do that, you have to create new patterns in your eating. Then you have to practice them until *they* become automatic.

To end overeating, you must retrain your brain so you can enjoy food and stay healthy at the same time. I know this is possible. I've done it myself, and I've seen other people do it, adults and teens.

To get started, it's good to remember some basic ideas we've discovered about overeating.

Food Fundamentals

1. Overeating doesn't happen because we are weak. It doesn't come from a lack of willpower. Overeating is primarily caused by the way sugar, fat, and salt work on our brains.

2. Foods loaded with sugar, fat, and salt are designed to get us hooked. They act on our brains the same way addictive drugs do.

3. Foods loaded with sugar, fat, and salt help create thoughts and urges that make us overeat and become overweight and obese. This leads to serious diseases like diabetes.

4. Foods loaded with sugar, fat, and salt do not satisfy hunger. They make us eat when we are not hungry. We can never really satisfy the urges for these foods.

5. We do not need to overeat. We may feel we want to eat, but that is not the same as needing to eat.

6. We are surrounded by powerful food cues that stimulate us to eat. Some of these cues are the ads and marketing campaigns of the food industry.

7. Overeating is a habit, a habit formed over time. Every time we go through the cycle of overeating, we make the habit stronger. We become conditioned overeaters.

8. We can retrain our brains to form new eating habits.

Enjoying Good Food

The most important thing you can do to retrain your brain is change the way you "see" food. You must understand that you do not need foods loaded with sugar, fat, and salt.

That doesn't mean you can never eat an ice-cream cone. It means you have to understand how that ice-cream cone works on your brain. You have to understand you don't *need* that ice-cream cone.

I'm not going to tell you to never eat an ice-cream cone or any other processed food. I will tell you that the most important thing you can do is discover other foods that you *enjoy* that are *good for you.*

You need to "want" something more than high-fat, high-sugar foods.

There is a whole world of delicious food that tastes great and does not make you overeat. It's true that foods like fruits and vegetables don't give you the rush that an ice-cream cone will give you. They do something better. They taste good and they make you feel full and satisfied. If you want to end overeating, you have to make these good foods your new eating habit.

It may seem impossible, but if you make new eating habits, you will begin to desire those loaded and layered foods less and less. You will no longer feel you "need" that ice cream or fried chicken. You might even decide you don't want to eat them. More importantly, you will be in control. You will decide what, when, and how you eat. You will have stopped being an overeater.

CHAPTER 25

A New Look at Food

The only way you can stop overeating is if you *want* to. That may seem obvious, but I want you to think about it. High-sugar, high-fat foods are very appealing. The hijack our brains. The first three parts of this book are all about how these foods act on our brains so we *crave* them.

Why would you give up something that tastes so good, something that makes you feel good?

Why? Because the truth is, this food may make you feel good for a few minutes, but that's not all it does to you. Take a step back and think about everything that happens when you eat these loaded and layered foods.

Think about it:

- Does the thought of being overweight or obese make you feel good or bad?
- Does being out of control with food make you feel good or bad?

- Do you really get satisfaction from these foods, or are you just eating all the time without thinking about it?
- Now that you know what is really in the food, do you want to be eating it?

High-sugar, high-fat foods might give us a few minutes of a "high." But those good feelings are often followed right away by feelings of sadness, anger, and despair. If you just think about the few minutes of feeling good, it is hard to break your previous learning. But if you remember all the ways overeating makes you feel bad, then you can begin to get some control. Then you can begin building new eating habits. This is the key to ending overeating.

☞ To end overeating, remember the ways that sugar, fat, and salt make us feel bad.

The Problem with Diets

Sometimes it seems like America is always on a diet. Added together, Americans probably lose millions of pounds every year. Even serious overeaters can go on a diet and lose weight, if they really try.

But then they gain it all back.

We don't gain the weight back because we are weak. We gain it back because we have not changed our habits. We have not retrained our brains. We are still conditioned overeaters. We have not changed how we think about food.

If you're an overeater, you probably have all sorts of feelings about food. You probably think of food as a reward—something that makes you feel good, or something you deserve. If you think of loaded and layered foods as delicious and great-tasting treats, then a diet makes you feel deprived. You spend a lot of energy denying yourself something good. This is very hard to do. In fact, it will just make your cravings worse. As we have seen, if you're an overeater and you feel bad about something, your first reaction is most likely to eat some loaded and layered food.

But what if you know that high-sugar, high-fat foods are tricking your brain? What if you know these foods don't really satisfy you, but just make you eat more? What if you know that the food industry wants to get you hooked so you will keep eating?

And what if you know that soon after you eat the food loaded with sugar, fat, and salt, you are going to feel miserable? If you understand all that, then you stop feeling that avoiding those foods is a hardship. You begin to feel that choosing foods not loaded and layered with sugar, fat, and salt is something good you are doing for yourself.

What Are Chicken Wings?

What do you see when you look at a plate of barbequed chicken wings? Do you see food that is very tasty that will make you feel good? Or do you see something loaded with sugar, fat, and salt that has been designed to make you overeat?

As you can see, there is more than one way to look at chicken wings. You can just think of the immediate feeling you'll get as you eat the wings. Or you can remember how you felt after you ate your last plate of wings. Did you feel satisfied? Did you even remember eating them? Did you immediately feel bad because you had "given in" once again?

When you look at those wings, or the ice-cream cone, or the pizza, it helps to look forward to what will happen after you eat. Don't just imagine how you will feel as you swallow. But how will you feel a few minutes after that? How will overeating make you feel? How will being overweight or obese make you feel?

Of course, this is not as easy as it sounds. The call of those wings is very strong. It is a powerful cue, urging you to eat. It will take some practice before you can pause for a second and remember everything that happens when you eat a plate of wings.

Anti-Smoking Lessons

People who want to stop smoking also have to retrain their brains. They often have strong emotions about smoking. Often they think of a cigarette as a reward, the same way an overeater thinks of a high-sugar, high-fat food as a reward. They may think that smoking is cool or makes them look attractive. And they smoke automatically, without thinking, the same way many overeaters eat.

To help them quit, smokers learn to change the way they think about cigarettes. They concentrate on the ways smoking makes them feel bad. They try to remember that cigarettes are unhealthy, smelly, and repulsive. Some smokers keep a jar full of old cigarette butts. When they feel like smoking, they stick their nose in the jar. The smell reminds them of the bad feelings they have about smoking. After enough practice, they stop thinking of cigarettes as a reward, as something that makes them feel good. They begin to have negative feelings about smoking, so it is easier to resist the urge to smoke.

At the same time, they begin to have positive feelings about not smoking. Instead of feeling that quitting is a hardship, they begin to feel good about it. Not smoking becomes a sort of reward, something that makes them feel good.

Quitting cigarettes is difficult because the nicotine in tobacco is an addictive drug. But in one way, quitting smoking is easier than giving up foods loaded with sugar, fat, and salt. That's because when you quit smoking, your aim is to stop smoking altogether. You can retrain your brain so you recognize that any kind of tobacco is bad.

But the solution to overeating isn't so simple. You can stop smoking, but you can't stop eating. So you have to learn the difference between foods that are good, satisfying, and healthy, and foods that just give you cravings to eat more. You have to retrain your brain so you quiet the cravings that make you overeat and instead enjoy the right amount of good, healthy food.

Emotions Are Stronger Than Ideas

To retrain your brain, it's not enough to know that high-sugar, high-fat foods are bad for you. Most people know that already.

Most people who are overweight or obese know it's unhealthy to be that way. They know they shouldn't eat that piece of chocolate cake. That's why so many overeaters have long debates in their brains. One part of the brain wants to stop overeating, and the other part has strong desires that make you overeat.

As we've seen, you can't win that debate in your brain as long as you feel that these loaded and layered foods are good. The emotional pull of the craving is too strong. You feel you are denying yourself something good, and that feels like a painful hardship. Only when you come to dislike what is really in the high-fat, high-sugar food you are eating can you begin to break the hold the food has on you.

This will be a slightly different process for each of us. Once, I thought a big plate of food was what I wanted and needed to feel better. Now I see that plate for what it is—layers of fat on sugar on fat that will never satisfy me and only keep me coming back for more. Now large portions look very different to me. I don't have good feelings about them. Instead, I feel they are something I don't want.

The same thing is true for many of the fatty, sugary foods I used to eat all the time. Today, I don't even want them. In fact, some of them seem disgusting to me now. I know that may seem impossible to you, but it's really true. It's not easy, but you *can* retrain your brain.

It can't happen by someone telling you to change. You have to change what you want.

CHAPTER 26

Taking Control

Overeaters feel out of control. We feel at the mercy of food cues—sights, smells, places that give us the urge to eat. These cues send us into a never-ending cycle that goes from cue to craving to eating.

To break the overeating cycle, first you have to be aware of your food cues. What are the things that give you the urge to eat? Where do you run into them during the day? Are they things you see or smell? Or are the cues a part of your daily routine, like a street you pass every day? Perhaps you just have a snack every day at the same time, so the time of day is your food cue.

We can try to avoid food cues. If your route to school takes you past a bunch of fast food restaurants, you can decide to walk a different way. But it's just not possible to avoid all the food cues in our lives. No matter how hard we try, we're getting dozens of food cues a day. High-sugar, high-fat food is everywhere; you just can't get away from it.

We can't get away from food cues, but we can learn to take away their power. To do that, you have to:

1. Recognize your food cues.

2. Understand how they work on you.

3. *Have a plan for dealing with your cues.*

4. Get support from friends and family.

5. Don't get discouraged.

This is not easy, but with practice you can do it.

☞ **You can take control of your eating by understanding your food cues and making a plan for dealing with them.**

Recognize Your Cues

Many overeaters eat without thinking about it. So all you have to do is start to *think* about when, where, and what you are eating. How often do you eat? What are you eating? Which foods do you crave? Most of all, you should try to recognize the moment when you get the urge to eat. Try to figure out the cue. There is always a cue.

What are your weak spots? Are they donuts, potato chips,

or so-called high-energy drinks? Are you eating extra meals, like a hamburger every day after school? Do you drink super-sized thirty-two-ounce sodas? Do you automatically take something out of the refrigerator whenever you go in the kitchen?

It's important to be able to recognize that very first moment when your desire is about to hit. That is the moment when your cycle of overeating is about to begin again. It's also the exact moment when you have a chance *to stop* the cycle. It's the moment when you have a choice. You can recognize what is about to happen and do something else instead.

Think of the cue as an invitation—an invitation to eat. If you recognize what is about to happen, you can decide not to accept the invitation. That is when you have to remind yourself about what is really happening.

You have to tell yourself:

I'm not hungry.

That's just part of my brain reacting automatically to a food cue.

That food has been designed to make me eat.

If I eat that, I won't be satisfied—I'll just want to eat more.

If I eat that, I will feel bad almost immediately.

Suppose you find yourself thinking, "That pint of chocolate ice cream looks really good to me; I'll have just a few bites." Instead, try saying this: "I know that once I start, I'll eat the whole thing, and then I will hate myself."

Of course, you don't have to say exactly these words. You should find the words that fit the way you feel. But you have to change the story you're telling yourself. The important thing is to look ahead a little and think about how you will feel *after* you eat that ice cream.

Each time you do this, you will build new patterns in your brain. And each time you do it, the food cue will become a little weaker, and your sense of control will become a little stronger.

Change Your Routine

Do you go straight to the refrigerator every time you come home from school? Change your routine and don't even go in the kitchen. If every time you sit down to watch TV you eat potato chips, switch to eating apples (or any other fruit you like). Instead of a sugar-filled high-energy drink, have plain water.

Whatever you do, be prepared. Once that food cue hits, you only have a moment to respond before the desire becomes too strong. So you have to plan in advance. You have to be ready with a different choice. The overeating cycle is like a railroad train coming down the track. If you don't do anything, the train will speed away down the same old track again. But if you act fast, you can switch it over to a different track. So you have to know what you're going to do before you even see the train coming.

It's important to remind yourself that you *do* have control. Tell yourself, "I don't have to eat that; I can do something else." Or tell yourself, "If I don't eat that now, I'll feel better about myself."

When you think this way, you are changing the whole debate in your head. You no longer feel you are denying yourself something you "need" or "deserve." Instead you begin to feel good because you are doing what you really want.

Get Support

None of this is easy. That's why it helps to have support, especially from family members. Also it is very hard to stop overeating if your friends and family are constantly offering you food.

You should tell your friends and family that you want to change your habits. They can help you out by encouraging you. Plus, just telling them gives you another reason to stick to your plans. You will want to succeed even more when you know that other people are behind you.

Once you begin talking about it, you might find that one or more of your friends or relatives has the same problem. If they also want to end overeating, you can support each other. Going through this process with someone else can make it a lot easier.

Don't Give Up!

Ending overeating is difficult. Remember, you have become conditioned to overeat after years of practice. You're not going to make your habits go away on your first try or even your tenth try. But it is very important that you *don't get discouraged*.

The first time you try to break your pattern, it may not work. You may wind up losing the argument with yourself. A lot of people have trouble at first. Don't get discouraged. Feeling bad and out of control will only make you want to eat more. Getting discouraged is a trap that leads to more overeating.

If you can't do it the first time, just remind yourself that you're up against a very strong habit. Think of what you did when you felt the urge to eat. Did you recognize what was happening? What did you say to yourself? How did you feel? Did you follow your plan? Think of ways to improve your plan. That will help you be ready the next time.

You may find that even if you have been successful for a while, you might slip. Maybe one day you find you just can't resist that old food. You wind up eating something you didn't want to eat. Don't get discouraged! This is also very normal. Habits like overeating form patterns in your brain. These patterns can last a long time. But if you follow your plan, the cravings will get weaker and weaker.

In place of your old eating habits, you can build up new patterns. When you pass your favorite donut shop, your conditioned response now might be something like "I really want one of those right now." But with practice, you can train yourself to think, "I used to eat those, but they made me feel bad afterward. I don't want one." Ultimately, you wouldn't even notice that you passed the donut shop.

Like anything else, it takes practice. The more you try, the more you will succeed. You *can* break the overeating habit.

CHAPTER 27

You Make the Rules

In the last chapter, I talked about making a plan for responding to food cues. One important part of making a plan is to make up your *food rules*. Rules are very helpful in stopping the cycle of overeating. They help change the debate in your head. Instead of arguing with yourself because you really want to eat something, you just remember the rule you made for yourself and follow it.

Rules help you deal with all the food cues you run into during the day. You can't avoid them all, and you can't plan for every single one. There are just too many. But if you have a set of food rules, then you're ready for any food cue.

These are rules that you make up yourself. They can be as simple as "I don't eat between meals." Or you can make a rule for a situation you know you're going to be in, like "I don't go into that Burger King after school."

☞ **Food rules should be part of your plan to stop overeating.**

Be Ready with Rules

When you first get that cue to overeat, you only have a split second. In that moment, you have to take control to stop the cycle of overeating. It's too late then to start thinking of what you should do. That's how rules help you take control. You can answer the automatic urge to eat donuts with a simple rule. If potato chips are your big weakness, you can say to yourself, "I don't eat potato chips anymore." Or you can make a rule for a time of day, like "I don't eat ice cream before supper." Or you can make a rule about portion sizes, like "I don't eat two helpings of mac and cheese." Simple rules are the best, like "I don't eat french fries," "I do not eat dessert."

When you say your rule, include a reason you don't want to overeat. For example, you can say, "I don't eat candy bars because I always eat too much and then I feel bad." A rule like that helps silence the urge because you are remembering that this food might make you feel good for a short time, but soon after you will feel bad.

Rules aren't the same thing as willpower. You aren't arguing against something you want. You're reminding yourself that you really don't want it. Just making the effort to take control can be very powerful. If you do it every time you feel the urge to overeat, you will find that the cravings begin to go away.

The Call of the Dumplings

Here's one of my rules: Every time I go through the San Francisco airport, I pass the food court. After long, painful experience, I've learned that just passing the food court is one of my food cues. I know that when I walk in that direction, I'll start thinking about dumplings. My brain goes on automatic. I see the food court, and I want to stop and eat dumplings, whether I'm hungry or not.

When the craving came on, I used to see the whole thing in my mind. I saw the dumplings; I saw myself stopping and wolfing them down. I imagined how good they would taste going down. The call of the dumplings was very powerful.

The problem is, I can't avoid going to the airport and passing the food court. That's why I need a rule, so I'll be prepared for that cue. My rule is very simple. I do not eat dumplings at the food court. I remind myself that what I'm feeling is just a reflex reaction. I don't need the dumplings, and as soon as I finish eating them I will feel rotten.

If I think of it that way, the decision becomes much easier. The debate in my brain goes away. Eating those dumplings won't make me feel good for more than a second. Then I will feel terrible. Why would I want to go through that again?

Every time I go to the airport, I remember my rule. I have to admit, even though I'm a doctor and had done a lot of research, I was surprised to find that this works. Having a rule makes it a lot easier for me to walk past that food court. I don't have to have a long, painful debate with myself. I just tell myself the rule and keep walking. Once I pass the food court, the urge dies down quickly.

I can't tell you that the urge for dumplings has gone away completely. I still feel it sometimes. But the call of the dumplings is much, much weaker. I am in control, not them.

You Can't Eat Just One

Another important rule you'll need is the one that says, "I can't eat just one because once I start I won't be able to stop." Overeaters tell themselves all the time. "I'll just have a bite," or "I'll just have a taste."

As I said earlier, this is a big trap. You may think you can stop after just one taste, but the first taste of a food is a powerful trigger that will drive you to eat more. That first taste increases your craving. It makes you want the food even more than you did before the first bite.

When you feel yourself tempted to have "just a bite," remember what happened last time. Were you able to stop after just one taste of cake or one small cookie? If you're like me, you probably went on to eat the whole slice of cake and then maybe another. If you had one cookie, you went on to eat three or four or even the whole box.

That's why you need a very clear rule. If you don't want to eat a food, then don't even taste it. Remember that you can't eat just one.

Make an Exercise Rule, Too

While you're making food rules, you should make an exercise rule, too. Exercise is one of the best things you can do to break the overeating cycle. Exercise burns calories, but it does something else, too. Regular exercise will help you control your urges to overeat. In fact, exercise can be a substitute for overeating.

Exercise stimulates the reward center in your brain, the same part of your brain that reacts to foods high in sugar, fat, and salt. That's why you feel better after you exercise. You may be tired, but most people say their mood is better and they are happier during the day if they have exercised.

If you are overeating to reward yourself and to help your mood, then exercise can take the place of that reward. Regular exercise also makes you feel better about yourself. You feel stronger, healthier, and more in control. By exercising every day, you prove to yourself that you can make good choices. And it's another way you can change your old habits and make new ones.

It's a great idea to substitute exercise for the things you do that make you overeat. Not only will you wind up with less "eating time," but the exercise will help you feel better. That will make it easier to stick to your food rules when you do play video games.

You don't need to become a marathon runner or an athlete to feel the benefits of exercise. If you haven't been exercising at all, then a short daily walk is enough to feel the difference. Don't stop there, though. You'll find the more you exercise, the more you will enjoy it and want to do it. The trick is to find something you like doing—whether it's a team sport or an activity like skateboarding or swimming or dancing. As long as you like doing it, you'll wind up exercising every day and feeling like a new person.

CHAPTER 28

Planned Eating

As you now know, our brains are wired to want sugar, fat, and salt. This brain wiring comes down to us from millions of years of evolution when our ancestors needed to find and remember high-calorie sources of food. Early humans 100,000 years ago couldn't overeat because there wasn't much high-calorie food available.

Today that has completely changed. High-calorie food is everywhere, and it is relatively inexpensive. Everywhere you go you see vending machines, convenience stores, supermarkets, and fast food restaurants of every kind. As a result, it is now possible to eat everywhere, all the time. The fact that food is available everywhere, anytime makes overeating possible.

That means we need a food rule about *when* we eat. That includes how many meals we eat, where we eat them, and what we do between meals.

☞ To get control over our lives, we have
to break the habit of nonstop eating.

Ten Meals a Day?

Today it seems that everyone eats all day long. And even though we eat during the day, we don't eat less when it's mealtime. For serious overeaters, it's like eating many meals a day.

Our eating habits are totally out of control. This unplanned eating helps make overeating possible. To stop overeating, you need to plan when and where you will eat. You need rules for this, and the rules should include things like:

- I eat at mealtimes.
- I know when I am going to snack.
- I don't eat while I'm doing something else, like watching TV.

I think of these as super rules. If you don't eat except when you plan to, you can use that rule to stop almost any food cue.

But these have to be *your* rules. They have to work for you. If you feel you need to have a snack after school, then you can include that in your rules. You could say something like "I eat one snack a day, at 4 p.m., and I know what I am going to have."

Eating with other people at a real meal is the best way to enjoy your food and not overeat. You should eat your meals at a dinner table or kitchen table. Wolfing down your food in front of the TV is not a meal.

CHAPTER 29

Just-Right Eating

You will also need to make a rule about how *much* food you will eat. Most overeaters think they need a lot more food than they do.

When I was working on this book, I talked to one of the top food coaches in the country. I told her everything I had eaten for dinner the day before. I thought I had not eaten too much, and I was proud of myself for skipping dessert. She had a different opinion. "You just ate twice as much as you needed," she told me.

I was stunned. I realized I had lost track of how much food I actually needed. Since then, I've worked hard to figure out how much I need. I call it "just-right eating." You want to eat enough so you feel satisfied, but not so much that you've gone past the point of feeling full.

☞ **Learn to eat enough to feel satisfied and full, but no more.**

Eat When You're Hungry

One thing you need to learn is the difference between being hungry and wanting to eat. Overeaters often say they're hungry, but what they really mean is they have an urge to eat. Being hungry is something else. If you're eating the right amount of food, you should feel hungry before mealtime. If you're an overeater, you may have forgotten what that feels like. You may go all day without actually being hungry.

How do you figure out how much food you really need? First make sure you have a firm plan for *when* you are going to eat during the day. If you want to have a snack, plan that, also. Then you have to experiment. A "just-right" meal should keep you feeling full for about four hours. A "just-right" snack should keep you feeling full for about two hours.

Before you sit down to a meal, you should have a very clear idea of how much you plan to eat. Many overeaters will eat whatever is put in front of them. This is why you need a rule about how much you will eat.

Enjoy Your Food

By now, you may be saying to yourself, "All these rules will take the fun out of eating." But ask yourself if you have really been enjoying your food. If you've been eating quickly without tasting it, if you've been eating automatically, then you can't be enjoying it. If you feel bad right after you eat, if overeating makes you feel bad about yourself, then you're not enjoying your food.

Believe it or not, eating real food will be more enjoyable than loaded-and-layered processed food. You may struggle for a while with cravings for foods with lots of sugar, fat, and salt, but it won't take very long to retrain your taste buds to appreciate the taste of real fruits, vegetables, grains, and meat.

You will learn which foods make you feel satisfied and full. Sugary foods give you a rush, but leave you feeling hungry very soon after. Whole vegetables, grains, and lean meats keep you feeling full much longer. What should you eat? That's up to you. The only eating plan that works is one that is full of foods you enjoy. Everyone is different.

Your Game Plan

You might think of all this as a game against a powerful opponent. You're not going to win every point. It will take a few rounds until you figure out your winning moves. You'll need a game plan. That means you have to think before every meal, and when you run into food cues during the day. What are you going to eat and how are you going to eat it? After a while, your game plan will become more automatic. You won't have to think so much about your response to food. It will become your new habit.

CHAPTER 30

Good Eaters

Eating is personal. Everyone has different tastes and preferences. I can't give you a strict set of rules to live by. You would quickly find them impossible to follow. The best plan for breaking the cycle of overeating is the one that you make for yourself, using advice from your doctor, this book, and other sources you trust.

You might find it useful to read about the eating rules of other people. Some of the things they do might work for you. Some might not.

All these people have one thing in common. They have thought about their food rules, and they have a plan for what, where, and how they will eat. Some just came to their plan naturally. Others had to work hard to figure it out. But today they all live without falling into the trap of overeating.

☞ Good eaters all have a plan for what,
where, and how they will eat.

Think Before You Eat

Remember Andrew, my friend who had so much trouble resisting M&Ms? Strangely, his wife has very different food habits. She does not have trouble resisting those M&Ms. She's a good example of someone who has great eating habits.

The two of them told me this story. One day, Penny and Andrew were driving somewhere and they were in a hurry. Penny said she was hungry, so Andrew suggested a fast stop at a gas station so she could pick up a candy bar. Penny told him not to bother.

"Even though I'm really hungry, I can't eat that," she explained. "It's not going to make me feel better. It's not going to satisfy me."

Penny didn't have to struggle with an inner voice that urged her to eat a candy bar. She knew that a candy bar would not satisfy her hunger. She only eats when she's hungry, and then she only eats real food. Put a plate of cookies before her, and she'll say, "No, thanks."

Penny's personal food plan includes a lot of protein. She'll often have a chicken salad or a turkey sandwich for lunch. Steak and salad is one of her favorite dinners. She doesn't bother to measure how much food she eats. Instead, she has learned to estimate the quantity that's right for her. She has simply figured out what to eat to feel satisfied, but not overstuffed. "I eat what my body needs to run," she says. "I know how food is going to make me feel."

Know What You're Eating

As you can see, Penny does something most of us do not. She makes her own set of rules, and then she follows them. Some of her rules might not work for you, but they work for her. They help her feel good about food. She never feels deprived, and she isn't denying herself something she wants. Instead, she feels she is eating what she really wants, not because of some craving.

Penny doesn't get her rules from a diet book or a magazine article. There's nothing wrong with getting ideas from books or magazines. In fact, I hope you get some ideas from this book. The point is, rules only work if they are *your* rules, the ones you understand and that fit your life.

I asked Penny how her food habits compare to Andrew's. One big difference, she said, is that she pays attention to what she is eating, and he doesn't. "Without even noticing, he puts the food in his hand and he eats it." But when food arrives at the table, Penny looks at it and says to herself, "Oh, there's food. Am I hungry? Is it good? Let me focus on it."

She always asks herself how eating something will make her feel. "Am I going to feel better off after I eat this? Am I going to be satisfied?" Such questions never seem to cross Andrew's mind.

Do You Want to Change?

Penny is lucky. She seems to have come up with her food rules naturally, without too much struggle. For many of us, deciding on our own food rules is more difficult.

Frank's story is very different from Penny's. He had struggled with weight since childhood. He was always a "fat kid," he says. Even as a child, he was an overeater who would eat frosting right out of the can. He would eat dinner at home and then go off to visit friends who ate later so that he could eat again.

By the time he reached his late twenties, Frank was seventy pounds overweight. But it was not just the weight that bothered him. One evening he sat alone eating an entire large pepperoni, mushroom, and green pepper pizza by himself. That's when he knew he had to change. Eating the pizza made him feel sick, but what scared him was feeling that he could not control his behavior.

That moment set Frank on a new course of action. He started writing his own food rules. He cut out all high-fat, high-sugar foods. He decided on three or four real food dinners he liked to eat and he stuck to them. He paid attention to portion sizes. He had rules about when he would eat during the day and made sure he ate just enough to get him to the next meal or snack. He also turned down dinner invitations if he thought his friends would serve food that was not in his plan.

Above all, Frank set up a routine and he stuck to it. "Put yourself into a routine, and you take away the temptation by not making it available," he explains.

There are two reasons Frank has been able to make this change in his life: First, he really wanted to change. Second, he feels good about his rules.

Frank's rules don't feel like a set of orders someone gave him to follow. They are *his* rules, ones that he made up. He doesn't feel as if he is keeping himself from something good. Instead, he feels that he is achieving something great. What also proved essential to him was viewing control of overeating as a personal challenge. Instead of being tortured with overeating cravings and out-of-control urges, he is enjoying food, maybe for the first time in his life.

Don't Diet—Enjoy Food

To many of us, going on a diet means starving or depriving ourselves of something we like. Diets don't last. That's why some weight loss specialists advise people to never say, "I'm on a diet." Instead, we should think of the new positive things we are doing to make ourselves feel good and enjoy our lives. These are rules we can follow happily for years to come.

Your food plan should make you feel good about food. Don't try to force yourself to eat something you don't like because it's "good for you." If you really don't like brussels sprouts, don't eat them. On the other hand, you may discover foods, like brussels sprouts, that you never tried before and you like. Those foods should go in your food plan.

Your food plan is not a punishment; it's a reward. It's your plan for a new, happier life with food.

CHAPTER 31

Your New Life with Food

I hope after all this you are ready to begin a new life with food. Changing your habits can be difficult, and you can't do it just because someone else tells you to. You have to really want to change. But if you *do* want to change, then you can.

Here are the basic guidelines you should remember:

1. Overeating doesn't happen because you are weak. Overeating is primarily caused by the way sugar, fat, and salt work on your brain.

2. You can retrain your brain so that you are in control of what, when, and how you eat.

3. You need a set of food rules that fit your life and your personal tastes.

4. Have a plan for what, when, and how you will eat.

5. When you feel a food craving for something you don't want to eat, imagine how you will feel a few minutes *after* you eat it.

6. Use any form of exercise as a substitute reward.

7. Learn to eat enough to feel satisfied and full, but no more.

8. Eat food you enjoy. You don't have to eat food you don't like.

9. If at first you have trouble keeping to your rules, don't get discouraged. It takes time to develop new learning.

I know from personal experience how hard it is to end overeating habits. As a doctor, part of my job is to give people advice on how to stay healthy. But for years, I found it very hard to follow my own advice. It was only after I researched and wrote this book that I found a new way to deal with overeating, one that works. I know it can also work for you.

Eating Is Good

I want to end by repeating something I said before: Eating is good. Eating is not only good for you, you can't live without it.

One of the signs of overeating is that we wind up tortured and tormented by food instead of just enjoying it. You will know you have begun to beat overeating when you stop worrying about food all the time.

Some people are afraid to change their food habits. They think that eating will be boring. But the truth is just the opposite. People who are not trapped in the cycle of overeating enjoy their food much more than overeaters. They know what they're eating and don't just eat automatically. They taste their food and get real satisfaction from it. My wish for you is that you learn to enjoy food that way.

Q & A WITH DR. KESSLER

What surprised you most while researching this book?

I wanted to understand why it was so hard to control what we eat. I thought the answer would have something to do with metabolism or how our bodies burn calories. Instead, I found the answer in the workings of the brain and inside the food industry.

My starting point was: Why did a chocolate chip cookie have such power over me? I didn't understand why my hand would reach for a cookie as if it had a mind of its own. Why did my hand start reaching before I even thought about it? Only when I understood how my brain works, what triggers my cravings for food, and the patterns that I've formed over years of eating, did I learn why food has that kind of power.

When I saw that woman on daytime TV who said she ate when she was hungry and when she was not hungry, when she was happy, and when she was sad, I wanted to understand what was driving her behavior. It was not just that she was eating too much—she was eating when she didn't want to eat. And nobody could explain why. I wanted to know: How could we help her?

What was driving her? The greatest surprise was learning how loaded and layered foods had hijacked her brain.

What role does the food industry play in overeating?

Food companies know what makes us crave certain foods, and they are able to design foods to trigger that craving. The food industry understands that sugar, fat, and salt stimulate our desire. They understand the result is we come back for more.

The food industry says they only give consumers what they want, meaning what tastes good. But they aren't selling just any commodity. They've designed highly stimulating products that trigger the reward center in our brains. Nothing sells as much as something that stimulates the reward center of the brain.

Of course, as consumers, we have to be responsible for what we buy and what we eat. Just because something is triggering a part of my brain, I still have the responsibility to figure that out and choose whether I will react or not. But the food industry also has a responsibility to not make products that drive us to overeat.

What percentage of Americans would you say suffer from overeating?

There's a range. For probably 15 percent of the population, and that's just a guess, food is not a very important part of their lives. You ask them, and they say, "I can eat or not. I have to eat in order to sustain myself, but it's not a large part of my life." That's a minority of people. But there are a lot of people who do not have natural self-control when it comes to food.

I would say about 70 million people would strongly identify with these three key characteristics: They have a sense of loss of control in the presence of loaded and layered food. They do not get a feeling of being full when eating loaded and layered foods. They spend a lot of time thinking about food between meals.

How can people become more aware of their food choices?
The fundamental question, when you look at food, is this: Is it real food, or is it food that is layered and loaded with sugar, fat, and salt? It's easy to look at food and see what is being layered on top. I don't have a problem with a plain hamburger—it's when you begin adding things like cheese and bacon. Also, you want a reasonable amount of food that you can control. Today if you put a large amount of food in front of me, I don't want it.

But I used to go through big portions in an instant. We each have to decide what we find rewarding and then decide how we control it.

As the former head of the U.S. Food and Drug Administration, what do you believe is the role government can or should play in this issue?
I think a good model is the way we dealt with tobacco use. Yes, the government regulates who can buy tobacco, but the most effective thing in stopping tobacco use has been changing the way people think about smoking. Through effective ads we have gotten people to stop thinking about tobacco as "something I want, that's glamorous, that's sexy." Instead we have gotten people to realize that "this is a deadly, disgusting product."

Our goal is to change how we view food. If we look at something and say, "That's going to make me feel good. I want that," our brains will drive us to get it. If we look at it and say, "Ugh, that's disgusting. I'd rather have something else," our brains aren't going to be stimulated in the same way. We have to take the power away from loaded and layered foods by changing how we view them. It's retraining the brain. You have to add new patterns on top of old learning—but you never get rid of that old learning, those old brain patterns.

Does this mean we should never treat ourselves to a chocolate chip cookie?

This is tricky. If you look at that cookie as a reward and you are depriving yourself of a reward, then you feel the cookie is really good, something you deserve, and that only makes you want it more. So that doesn't work. We need to decide what foods actually make us feel good and then have a plan that helps us control our behavior. So if I get cued and my brain gets activated, I can say, "I don't want that now because I'm going to have something else later that I want more."

High-sugar, high-fat foods have always been around—our grandmothers baked cookies, too—but there was always a limit to them. That kind of food was an occasional reward. Now all eating has become rewarding, so we need rules or we will eat all the time.

Of course, there's a certain percentage of people who are eating in balance, and it's important to note that this issue doesn't necessarily apply to them. They can eat a cookie or two and walk away. But for the rest of us who do have a hard time controlling what we eat, we need to change the way we look at food. We need to be able to look at food and say, "That's nutritious; that's going to make me feel good; I'm going to feel good after I eat that." Or we need to look at that food and say, "That may taste good for a couple of seconds, but I'm not going to like myself in twenty minutes if I eat that." The way you think and feel about the food can define your behavior to a great extent.

ACKNOWLEDGMENTS

The End of Overeating was the work of many years. Without the efforts of Karyn Feiden, Julie Will, Dick Todd, and Kathy Robbins the book would never have come to be. This terrific adaptation for young readers by Richie Chevat gives me the opportunity to thank again the many other individuals who offered their expertise, friendship, insight, and support in the creation of *The End of Overeating*: Jeff Goldberg, Al Gore, Steven Murphy, Joe Klein, Karen Rinaldi, Yelena Nesbit, Aly Mostel, Nancy N. Bailey, Beth Davey, Christina Gaugler, Beth Lamb, Chris Jerome, Richard Alwyn Fisher, Cal Johnson, Harry Slomovits, Josh Marx, Bob Marsh, Megan O'Neill, Jennifer Hornsby, Erana Bumbardatore, Nancy Rutman, Deb Reiter, Chip Kidd, Jerry Mande, Elizabeth Drye, Nick Gimbel, Brooke Shearer, Mathea Falco, Joel Ehrenkranz, Connie Casey, Lynn Gryll, Ruth Katz, Nina Questal, Ann Litt, Marci Robinson, Jeff Nesbit, Jim O'Hara, Sharan Jayne, Drew Altman, Tina Hoff, Doug Levy, Elissa Epel, Dana Small, Andras Hajnal, Jeffrey Grimm, Dianne Figlewicz, Jennifer Felsted, Gaetano Di Chiara, Michael Acree, Dina Halme, Tanya Adams, Stewart Resnick, Lynda Resnick, Marc Benioff, Lynne Benioff, Lionel Pincus, and Keith Yamamoto.

Thanks are due to my son Ben Kessler, my daughter and

son-in-law Elise and Mike Snyder, and my parents Roz and Irv Kessler.

And—Paulette, wise counsel and wife, whom I've loved since Amherst snack bar days, I'll be downstairs in a minute.

Index

Hunger: conditioning to eat and, 50–51, 112, 116–119; eating to satisfy, 8, 37, 46, 78–81, 91; normal eating and, 5, 8, 18; super-stimuli foods, 20–21, 38–40; wanting to eat and hunger, difference between, 158; worldwide problem of, 90

I
Ingredients listings on labels, 84

M
Meals: planned eating, 155–156, 159; snacking instead of eating meals, 114
Memories. *See* emotions, memories, and food

N
Neurons, 42–43, 113

O
Obese and obesity: definition of, 4; health problems related to, 4, 9–10, 108; increase in, 12–13; number of kids who are, 10, 13; number of people who are, 4, 5, 9; overeating and, 105–110; overweight compared to, 10–11; worldwide expansion of, 89–90
One bite or just a taste, trap of, 34, 40–41, 119–120, 152–153
Opioids (endorphins), 43–45
Overeating: characteristics of overeaters, 107, 170; control over desire to eat, 14–15, 33–36, 71, 107, 125; definition of, 3–4, 5, 105–106; end of, 8; feelings about, 3–4, 136–141, 147, 158–159, 167–168; food effects on brain and, 42–46, 111–113, 116–123, 127–128, 131, 169–170; government role in changing, 171; habit of, 5–6, 54–57, 80, 122–123, 125, 132, 133; increase in, 76–77; kids who overeat, 108–110; nature or nurture,

113; number of people overeat, 170; problem for kids, 5–6, 71; signs of, 105–110; stimulus to overeat, 20–25, 42–43, 54–55, 111–113, 123–124; wanting to stop, 136, 141; weight gain and, 105, 106; why people overeat, 4–5, 7–8, 111–115, 132–133

Overeating cycle: diets and, 127–128; finding a way out, 126–128, 167–168; food cues and habits, 116–120, 122–123, 124, 133, 142–146; getting trapped in, 122–125; guidelines for changing habits, 166–168; steps in, 116–121; support to stop, 146

Overweight: health problems related to, 9–10, 108; increase in, 12–13; number of kids who are, 10, 13; number of people who are, 4, 5, 9; obese compared to, 10–11; overeating and, 105–110

P

Pizza and pizza restaurants, 31, 73, 74, 88, 163

Portions, 6, 8, 46, 100–102, 171

Potato chips, 86, 120

Processed and restaurant foods: artificial flavors and chemicals, 91–94, 101; attitudes toward, changing, 171–172; cost of, 91, 93, 100–101, 102; design and selling of so we want more, 7–8, 14, 26–31, 54–57, 61–71, 78–81, 100–102, 169–170; food carnival, 47–53, 112, 171; increase in amount being eaten, 77, 115; mass-produced and pre-cooked food, 95–98; mouthfeel, 69–70; perfect food, 95–98; as stimulus to overeat, 20–25, 42–43, 54–55, 123–124; testing new products, 82–86

R

Reinforcing foods, 37–41

ABOUT THE AUTHOR

David A. Kessler, MD, served as commissioner of the US Food and Drug Administration under presidents George H. W. Bush and Bill Clinton. He is a pediatrician and has been dean of the medical schools at Yale and the University of California, San Francisco. A graduate of Amherst College, the University of Chicago Law School, and Harvard Medical School, Dr. Kessler is the father of two and lives with his wife in California.